CW01263092

The Real Peter Sellers

By the Same Author

By Swords Divided: Corfe Castle in the Civil War. Halsgrove, 2003
Thomas Hardy: Christmas Carollings. Halsgrove, 2005
Enid Blyton and her Enchantment with Dorset. Halsgrove, 2005
Tyneham: A Tribute. Halsgrove, 2007
Agatha Christie: The Finished Portrait. Tempus, 2007
The Story of George Loveless and the Tolpuddle Martyrs. Halsgrove, 2008
Father of the Blind: A Portrait of Sir Arthur Pearson. The History Press, 2009
Agatha Christie: The Pitkin Guide. Pitkin Publishing, 2009
Arthur Conan Doyle: The Man behind Sherlock Holmes. The History Press, 2009
HMS Hood: Pride of the Royal Navy. The History Press, 2009
Purbeck Personalities. Halsgrove, 2009
Bournemouth's Founders and Famous Visitors. The History Press, 2010
Thomas Hardy: Behind the Mask. The History Press, 2011
Hitler: Dictator or Puppet? Pen & Sword Books, 2011
A Brummie Boy goes to War. Halsgrove, 2011
Winston Churchill: Portrait of an Unquiet Mind. Pen & Sword Books, 2012
Charles Darwin: Destroyer of Myths. Pen & Sword Books, 2013
Beatrix Potter: Her Inner World. Pen & Sword Books, 2013
T.E. Lawrence: Tormented Hero. Fonthill, 2014
Agatha Christie: The Disappearing Novelist. Fonthill, 2014
Lawrence of Arabia's Clouds Hill. Halsgrove, 2014
Jane Austen: Love is Like a Rose. Fonthill, 2015
Kindly Light: The Story of Blind Veterans UK. Fonthill, 2015
Thomas Hardy at Max Gate: The Latter Years. Halsgrove, 2016
Corfe Remembered. Halsgrove, 2017
Thomas Hardy: Bockhampton and Beyond. Halsgrove, 2017
Mugabe: Monarch of Blood and Tears. Austin Macauley, 2017
Making Sense of Marilyn. Fonthill, 2018
Hitler's Insanity: A Conspiracy of Silence. Fonthill, 2018
The Unwitting Fundamentalist. Austin Macauley, 2018
Robert Mugabe's Lost Jewel of Africa. Fonthill, 2018
Bound for the East Indies: Halsewell – A Shipwreck that Gripped the Nation. Fonthill, 2020
Beatrix Potter: Her Inner World. Pen & Sword Books, 2020
The Amazing Story of Lise Meitner: Escaping the Nazis and Becoming the World's Greatest Physicist. Pen & Sword Books, 2021

The Real Peter Sellers

A Candid Biography of a Comic Genius

Andrew Norman

WHITE OWL

First published in Great Britain in 2021 by
White Owl
An imprint of
Pen & Sword Books Ltd
Yorkshire – Philadelphia

Copyright © Andrew Norman 2021

ISBN 978 1 52678 683 8

The right of Andrew Norman to be identified as Author of this work has been asserted by him in accordance with the Copyright, Designs and Patents Act 1988.

A CIP catalogue record for this book is
available from the British Library.

All rights reserved. No part of this book may be reproduced or transmitted in any form or by any means, electronic or mechanical including photocopying, recording or by any information storage and retrieval system, without permission from the Publisher in writing.

Typeset by Mac Style
Printed and bound in the UK by CPI Group (UK) Ltd,
Croydon, CR0 4YY.

MIX
Paper from
responsible sources
FSC
www.fsc.org   FSC® C013604

Pen & Sword Books Limited incorporates the imprints of Atlas, Archaeology, Aviation, Discovery, Family History, Fiction, History, Maritime, Military, Military Classics, Politics, Select, Transport, True Crime, Air World, Frontline Publishing, Leo Cooper, Remember When, Seaforth Publishing, The Praetorian Press, Wharncliffe Local History, Wharncliffe Transport, Wharncliffe True Crime and White Owl.

For a complete list of Pen & Sword titles please contact

PEN & SWORD BOOKS LIMITED
47 Church Street, Barnsley, South Yorkshire, S70 2AS, England
E-mail: enquiries@pen-and-sword.co.uk
Website: www.pen-and-sword.co.uk

Or

PEN AND SWORD BOOKS
1950 Lawrence Rd, Havertown, PA 19083, USA
E-mail: Uspen-and-sword@casematepublishers.com
Website: www.penandswordbooks.com

Contents

About the Author   vii
Acknowledgements   viii
Author's Note   ix
Preface   xi

Chapter 1	Who Was Peter Sellers?	1
Chapter 2	Sellers and His Father 'Bill'	4
Chapter 3	Sellers and His Mother 'Peg'	6
Chapter 4	Sellers Embarks on a Career	10
Chapter 5	Wife Number One: Anne Aspinwall-Howe (Married to Sellers 1951–1963)	16
Chapter 6	Wife Number Two: Britt Ekland (Married to Sellers 1964–1968)	23
Chapter 7	Wife Number Three: Miranda Quarry (Married to Sellers 1970–1974)	28
Chapter 8	Ambition: Talent: Humility	31
Chapter 9	Getting into the Mindset of His Characters	33
Chapter 10	Sellers' Wonderful Sense of Humour	35
Chapter 11	The Real Peter Sellers	37
Chapter 12	Sellers' Core Beliefs	42
Chapter 13	Generosity and Acts of Kindness	56
Chapter 14	Nostalgia	59
Chapter 15	Some Notable Film and Stage Appearances	61

Chapter 16	Insecurity and the Need to Escape	64
Chapter 17	Low Self-Esteem and its Possible Origins	66
Chapter 18	Sellers and Religion	70
Chapter 19	Sellers and Superstition	71
Chapter 20	Sellers and the Paranormal	75
Chapter 21	Sellers and Spiritualism	78
Chapter 22	Was Sellers Insane? A Personality Disorder?	82
Chapter 23	Possible Origins of Sellers' Personality Disorder	90
Chapter 24	A Rollercoaster of Joy and Despair	95
Chapter 25	Why Sellers Could Not Be Happy for Any Length of Time	99
Chapter 26	*Being There*	103
Chapter 27	*Being There* and its Significance for Sellers	113
Chapter 28	Wife Number Four: Lynne Frederick (Married to Sellers 1977–1980)	119
Chapter 29	The Death of Sellers: Aftermath	124
Chapter 30	In Conclusion	128
Notes		133
Bibliography		147
Index		148

About the Author

Andrew Norman was born in Newbury, Berkshire in 1943. Having been educated at Thornhill High School, Gwelo, Southern Rhodesia (now Zimbabwe), Midsomer Norton Grammar School, and St Edmund Hall, Oxford, he qualified in medicine at the Radcliffe Infirmary. He has two children, Bridget and Thomas, by his first wife.

From 1972 to 1983, Andrew worked as a general practitioner in Poole, Dorset, before a spinal injury cut short his medical career. He is now an established writer whose published works include biographies of Charles Darwin, Winston Churchill, Thomas Hardy, T.E. Lawrence, Adolf Hitler, Agatha Christie, Enid Blyton, Beatrix Potter, Marilyn Monroe, and Sir Arthur Conan Doyle. Andrew married his second wife Rachel in 2005.

Author's website: www.andrew-norman.co.uk

Acknowledgements

I would like to thank Darin Ball, Peter Bass, Barry King, Ivor McNeill, Robert Norcliffe, and Bill Parnell. I am especially grateful to my beloved wife Rachel.

Author's Note

I happened to mention to an acquaintance of mine as we were having a coffee together in our favourite café in Poole (situated on the south coast of England) that I was considering writing a biography of Peter Sellers. He leaned back in his chair, smiled, and declared, 'He was a very complex character.'

This was Bill Parnell, picture editor and sound editor (now retired), who had worked on no less than ninety-four films as a freelance. This was at London, Shepperton, MGM, Associated British Pictures, and Pinewood Studios, under for example US directors John Huston and Alfred Zinnemann and British directors Lewis Gilbert and John Irvin. These films included *Aliens* (1986) and *Greystoke: The Legend of Tarzan, Lord of the Apes* (1984). Significantly, however, Bill had worked on *The Fiendish Plot of Dr Fu Manchu* (1980), which is where he first met Peter Sellers. (This was to be Sellers' final film.)

Much of what I had read about Sellers was confirmed by Bill. For example, 'He could mimic any accent.' Also, said Bill, 'He often responded to telephone calls, including those from across the Atlantic, by mimicking the accent of the caller.'

When the film *The Fiendish Plot of Dr Fu Manchu*, in which Sellers plays the part of the eponymous doctor, was almost completed, said Bill, Sellers approached him and told him that he thought there was something wrong with his performance, but could not pinpoint what it was. Whereupon Bill said that, in his opinion, Sellers needed to 'speed up'. 'Old people may talk with a quavering voice,' he said, 'but they do not usually speak slowly.' Sellers took this on board and at his insistence, and at great expense, parts of the film were re-shot!

When, one day, a lady arrived at the studios wearing a purple coat, said Bill, Sellers screamed at her to 'get out!' He was superstitious of the colours green and purple. This was 'after he met a medium who told him to avoid those colours as they would be very unlucky for him'.

Medium: a person claiming to be able to communicate between the dead and the living.[1]

On one occasion, Bill admired some photographs which Sellers, a keen amateur photographer, had taken himself. Whereupon, Sellers offered him his Swedish 'Hasselblad' camera, which in those days was priced at about £7,000, not including the lenses. Bill refused the offer, not wishing to take advantage of Sellers' typical generosity.

When Sellers arrived at the studio each morning, said Bill, 'You never knew who was coming: it all depended on his mood. When he could not get his own way, he would flare up, have a tantrum, rush away and then come back a few minutes later having calmed down.'

Sellers was only at ease with those he knew he could trust, said Bill. Also, unlike with many actors and directors, he did not interfere in the film-editing process. 'Whereas he normally resented criticism, when he was with his "own" people i.e. people such as the "Goons", he felt that they were exactly on the same wavelength. They would tease him unmercifully, "taking the mickey" by saying things like, "What car did you come in today, Peter?"'

'Sellers loved the feedback from a live audience: he loved their laughter, and he knew how to make them laugh,' said Bill. However, as a film star, this pleasure was denied him. Finally, he always came on the set immaculately dressed.

Preface

My interest in Peter Sellers began in 1959 when my uncle, David Waldin, gave me a gramophone record for my seventeenth birthday. It was entitled *Songs for Swingin' Sellers*.[1] When I played it, I was reduced to hysterical laughter. Sellers appeared to poke fun at virtually everything which, as a child, I had been taught to respect: the establishment, the rich and powerful, politicians. In fact, his attitude entirely chimed with that prevalent in the post-war era, where it was OK to 'have fun' and be disrespectful to one's 'elders and betters'. To my mind, this album, together with *The Best of Sellers*,[2] which had been released in the previous year, 1958, gives a unique insight into the mindset of Peter Sellers himself, and how he detested humbug, hypocrisy, and pretentiousness.

Although Sellers did not write the lyrics for the tracks for these two albums, the fact that he was prepared to take on the roles involved, and play them with such conviction, demonstrated that satire was a subject very close to his heart.

> Satire: The use of humour, irony, exaggeration, or ridicule to expose and criticise people's stupidity or vices. Irony: The expression of meaning through the use of language signifying the opposite typically for humorous effect.[3]

This was a characteristic of his which, of course, endeared him to those of a rebellious nature! Furthermore, no subject was beyond the scope of his mimicry: for example, the aristocracy, the rich and famous, politicians, so-called 'celebrities'. For he could impersonate people from all walks of life, both male and female, from a peer of the realm to a waitress!

Peter Sellers was born in 1925. He was therefore aged 34 and 35 respectively when *The Best of Sellers* was released in 1958, and *Songs for Swingin' Sellers* was released in 1959. These albums must be played and carefully listened to if Sellers' amazing versatility is to be fully appreciated.

Like millions of others, no doubt, I found Sellers' ability to mock, but in a humorous way, immensely appealing, and his two albums represent satire at its most cutting and sublime. And by adding the ingredient of humour, this made the satire even more powerful. Two tracks in particular, from *Songs for Swingin' Sellers*, stand out in my mind:

'*The Contemporary Scene – 1: Lord Badminton's Memoirs*'

Here, Sellers ridicules the aristocratic Lord Badminton for pretending that the welfare of his employees was of concern to him, whereas in fact he had a total disregard for them and held them in utter contempt!

'*The Contemporary Scene – 1: The Critics*'

Here, Sellers lampoons the arts critics, such as those who made regular appearances on BBC radio and television in the 1950s.

In the view of the author, these two albums should be part of the national curriculum of every country in the world, for they teach people of all ages, who may be under the mistaken impression that all human beings are honest, genuine, altruistic, and naturally kind and generous, how to recognise falseness and insincerity, whatever its source may be.

Towards the end of his life, Sellers would attack something else that he detested, viz. the materialism of western society, and he would do this vicariously, in the film *Being There*, as will be seen.

A second magic moment in my life in respect of Peter Sellers was when I was up at Oxford with my fellow undergraduate Robert: we went to see the film *The Pink Panther* at the Scala Theatre, Walton Street (now renamed The Phoenix). That was in 1964, the film having been released the previous year. In the film, which was written and directed by US film-maker Blake Edwards, with theme music composed by Henry Mancini, Sellers played the French detective, Inspector Jacques Clouseau.[4]

From that day forward, the persona of Inspector Clouseau entered into our very DNA. No longer was it possible for us to say certain words without feeling impelled to use 'Sellerian' intonations. Thus the 'phone' became the 'phown', 'bomb' became 'bumb' and whenever anything went wrong in our lives, we would say to each other ruefully and tongue in cheek, 'All our actions are planned!'

Chapter 1

Who Was Peter Sellers?

Sellers as an enigma

Said Spike Milligan, although it is Sellers the person, not Sellers the actor that interests us, 'the real Peter Sellers would have vanished long before anyone gets too close. Perhaps the enigma is more real than the man himself'.[1]

A non-existent personality?

In 1978, in a guest appearance on the US comedy television series the *Muppet Show* (aired in the UK on 1 January), Sellers stated that it would be 'altogether impossible' for him to relax and be himself. 'I could never be myself you see. There is no "Me". I do not exist. There used to be me, but I had it surgically removed.' At this the audience laughed, but there was a very serious underlying message. In his biography of his father, entitled *P.S. I Love You* (1981), Michael Sellers gave a first-hand account. Said he of his father, 'He was lost in himself [i.e. he was lost when he tried to be himself] because when you turned him off there wasn't anything there.'[2]

A mystery to himself?

Welsh comedian, actor, and singer Harry Secombe stated that he was 'always amazed' at Sellers' impersonations, 'yet when he was called upon to do his own natural voice, he was always worried. "I can't, lads", he'd say. "I don't know what I sound like".'[3]

Said Roger Lewis, author of *The Life and Death of Peter Sellers*, 'With Sellers he was so insecure he was vulnerable, he didn't know who he was from day to day.' Said actor and friend Simon Williams, 'I think he was an unhappy, miserable sort of man because I think he'd lost track of who he really was.'[4]

Said Sellers of himself, 'The only problem is we can't find him. I've been looking round all over the place. That microphone, that wouldn't be him down there would it? Just a moment, I'm not sure. Come on out of there! We know you're in there! No, no, no, he's not in there, no. That's stretching it a bit far for him in the nicest possible way.'[5] And when he was asked if there was a 'real Peter Sellers', he replied, 'I'm not the real Peter Sellers. I am in fact a mock-up, a plastic mock-up. Another copy of myself I leave at home, to do the housework.'[6]

An admixture of other people?

Said Sellers' biographer and friend Peter Evans, 'Anyone that he got close to he would steal from, and that in the end was the sum total of Peter Sellers – a collection of small parts from other people.'[7]

In the film *Being There*, where Sellers acts the part of a gardener called Chance, Evans continued, 'he plays this blank ordinary nothing of a man. He just lives his life by copying bits of behaviour that he's seen on the television screen, a man whose life is just duplicating bits and pieces that he's seen and that was the real Sellers.'

Thomas Wiseman was a reporter for the *Evening Standard*. In early 1959, he quoted Sellers as saying, 'Max Bygraves is Max Bygraves. But who am I? I don't exist. With me as myself, I might be some third-rate thing Carroll Levis (the talent scout) dug up. I can't move. I can't talk. I'm a very odd bod. I only exist as the various characters I create. They are more than me.'[8]

Could Sellers take an acting role in which he had to play himself?

The answer is no. Said he, 'I'd have probably very little confidence in myself if I thought that, well, I have to go there and act out myself. I don't know what I am. Oh God, I wouldn't know what to do.'[9]

A fairly ordinary bloke?

Said Roger Lewis, 'The trouble with Peter Sellers was that underneath all these baroque performances that he gave, he was actually rather ordinary and plain and blank, a bit of a mister nobody really.'[10]

Was Sellers ever 'himself'?

In 1978, Sellers starred alongside his new bride Lynne Frederick in *The Prisoner of Zenda*, in which he played several roles. Said Simon Williams, who played 'Fritz' in the film, 'He'd present a different person quite a lot of the time. Sometimes he'd come in and be a posh Sellers, or sometimes a Cockney Sellers, or a "Clouseau" Sellers, and that was even before he got on the set. And you'd think, who are you?'

The question is, therefore, is it true that Sellers as a personality did not exist as himself, and that he was only able to exist vicariously when acting the part of another? This will be discussed shortly.

Chapter 2

Sellers and His Father 'Bill'

William 'Bill' Sellers (original name 'Sellars') was born in 1900 in Bradford, Yorkshire. When Bill met his wife to be, Agnes Doreen 'Peg' Marks in 1921, he was resident pianist at the King's Theatre, Portsmouth, where she was appearing in a play entitled *More Splashes*.[1] They were married in London in 1923. 'Auntie Peg married Bill Sellers, who was the musical director of one of the shows,' said Sellers' cousin Dick Ray.[2]

Bill Sellers had started life as a tenant farmer, but as regards his subsequent life, it is not easy to distinguish fact from fiction. It was alleged that he had served in the Royal Navy during the First World War, played cricket for Yorkshire, served in the Merchant Navy in the Second World War, and taught actor, singer-songwriter, and comedian George Formby to play the ukulele.

Bill came from a working-class Yorkshire home, said Sellers' son Michael, 'in which family discipline was strong. From childhood he had taken piano lessons and music became his life's passion. He was still a young man when he was appointed organist at Bradford Cathedral.'[3] How much of this was true? In his biography of Sellers, Roger Lewis states that he was unable to verify any of these so-called 'facts'.[4]

What is known, however, is that as Michael stated, both Bill and his wife Peg became 'seasoned vaudeville troupers',[5] and that Bill played the ukulele in a singing duo in a review called *The Side Show*. The show was staged by the Ray brothers, sons of Sellers' maternal grandmother, Ma Ray.

In 1924, the year before Sellers was born, Peg had given birth to a stillborn son, whose name was to have been Peter. Said Roger Lewis, 'I think all the baby clothes were still around, kept in tissue paper, all rather morbid.' When her next child was born on 8 September 1925, he was given the name Richard Henry Sellers, 'but his mother called him Peter because this was like a replacement child.'[6]

According to Michael, Sellers had 'made his theatrical debut, being proudly held aloft by Bill on the King's theatre stage for the approval of the audience, who sang "For He's a Jolly Good Fellow".' This was only two weeks after his birth, on 8 September 1925.[7] Sellers subsequently progressed to playing minor parts on the stage, said Lewis.

Interviewed by broadcaster, journalist, and author Michael Parkinson in 1974, Sellers said that it was his father who taught him to play the banjo. Said Dick Ray, Sellers 'took the musical technicalities from his father and once he was on stage his mother's strength and personality came out.'[8]

It was at the Devonshire seaside resort of Ilfracombe in late 1939, said Lewis, that Sellers learnt to play the drums and perform in his father's band.[9] Bill had recognised his son's talents as a drummer, said US film scholar, author, and Sellers' biographer Ed Sikov, and in 1943, he formed a quartet, with Sellers on percussion using a set of drums that his father had purchased for him.[10]

By all accounts, Bill was quiet and retiring. Said Dick Ray, 'Peg dominated the family and Bill Sellers was a quiet, gentle man who wouldn't say boo to a goose.'[11] Said Michael, 'Unlike the more dominant and animated Peg,' Bill was 'modest, quiet and shy, prepared to play a supporting role which he uncomplainingly fulfilled throughout his lifetime.'[12] He was 'an easy going man, but not a force in my father's life, which was a shame.'[13]

Said Sellers to Parkinson, 'I used to travel round with my mother and father all over the country when I was a kid'.[14] Sometimes, however, said Sellers' biographer Alexander Walker, when Sellers' parents were touring, he was left at home. 'Then Ma Ray and Aunty Cissie [Ma Ray's sister] fussed over him. Bill Sellers had very little say in this matriarchal nest.'[15]

Another factor to be considered was that Bill, as a 'vaudeville trouper',[16] was often absent from home for weeks or months at a time, and there were other times when he deliberately chose to live separately from the family.

> Vaudeville: an entertainment in the early twentieth century featuring a mixture of musical and comedy acts.[17]

For example, said Sellers's first wife Anne, when Peg and Bill split up, albeit temporarily, in 1936, 'Peter was still very young, and so there was very little male influence in his life.' He and his mother now resided at 10 Muswell Hill Road, and his father Bill in Holloway.[18]

Chapter 3

Sellers and His Mother 'Peg'

Sellers' mother 'Peg' was born Agnes Doreen Marks in 1892 in Hackney, London. Her mother's maiden name was Benvenida Mendoza, and her nickname was 'Welcome'. When Benvenida married a London merchant called Solomon Marks, she became known as 'Ma Ray'. By 1911 'she had 40 vaudeville companies performing the length and breadth of England'.[1] And it was subsequently with Ma Ray's companies that her daughter Peg and Peg's husband Bill Sellers toured.

Following the marriage of Peg and Bill in 1923, Peg's next role was to travel the Home Counties with the young Peter in tow, buying and selling antiques.[2]

Said Sellers to Parkinson, 'My mum very much wanted me to go into the theatre' and thereby continue the family tradition. 'My [maternal] grandmother [Ma Ray] was in the theatre as well you see. Mum used to get up there in white tights, a rather daring thing in those days, and they used to project slides on to Mum and she would depict various famous characters from history as the slides changed. And my dad would play the old joanna [piano] in the front there.'[3] Said Secombe, Peg specialised in '"tableaux" with her pianist husband as her accompanist'.[4]

> Tableau: A group of models or motionless figures representing a scene.[5]

Said Dick Ray, 'Throughout Peter's early years he would have stood in the wings, watched the posing acts as we called it. Don't forget, between 1925 and 1935 it was very adventurous, Peg being in what we now call a leotard. It was unheard of. You didn't even go on the beach in a costume like that.'

'The family was on the road with the shows. They were travelling around the country with our grandmother, Ma Ray, who had a touring review which was a complete show with 24 dancing girls, comedians, singers, speciality acts. One of them was called "Splash Maids", with a huge aquatic tank on stage with girls diving in and swimming in unison and in patterns.' On one occasion the tank broke and flooded the orchestra pit![6]

When Ma Ray died in 1932, Bill and Peg commenced work with other troupes.[7] Subsequently, said Dick Ray, the travelling shows gradually diminished, but Bill Sellers remained on the boards with his ukulele act. He now saw less and less of his wife and son.[8]

Said film actor, director, and producer Bryan Forbes, who had directed *The Wrong Box* (1966) in which Sellers played Dr Pratt, 'Peg was the archetypal Jewish mother. Peg was the prime influence in Peter's life, both positively and negatively, and there was a thin dividing line between love and hate, the relationship.' And because of his mother's itinerant lifestyle, he was constantly moving house and changing schools.[9]

Spike Milligan first met Sellers at the Hackney Empire theatre in late 1949.[10] He described Sellers' relationship with his mother Peg as being 'rather unpleasant'. Sellers, he said, 'would call out to his mother for some breakfast first thing in the morning'.[11] 'They seemed to kiss over-affectionately and, first thing in the morning, he had a whining voice. When he woke up he'd say, "Peg! Peg!" "What is it, darling?" "Can I have some tea please?" "Yes, darling".[12] I realised that he was doomed from a heart attack through sheer lack of activity.'[13]

Comedian, actor, writer, and director Graham Stark first met Sellers in 1945, at the Gang Show's headquarters in Houghton Street, London. Sellers, he said, 'was an only child, but it was an absurd only child in the sense that the world revolved, in her [Peg's] eyes, around him. She literally worshipped him.'[14] Said Walker, when Sellers was a child, he 'he even slept in the same room as Peg, while Bill slept outside'.[15] Bill slept in a separate bedroom or on the couch and not, presumably, in the garden!

Michael described how this mollycoddling had a deleterious effect on his father's development. 'Peg could only blame herself for Dad's inconsiderate attitude. She had always given way to his demands as a child. Whatever misdemeanour he [Sellers] committed, he was forgiven.'[16]

Bert Mortimer first met Sellers in January 1961, when he became Sellers' chauffeur.[17] When Sellers joined the RAF in 1943, said Mortimer, his mother 'chose to be near him. She moved down to the barracks, wherever it was, and she took a bed and breakfast place nearby. Very embarrassing. She would be actually at the gates. Very possessive, Peg.'[18]

It was because she 'openly conspired to sabotage' her son's new friendship with his girlfriend, a blonde, said Michael, that in late April 1950, Sellers left the family's 'tiny, cluttered three-roomed flat at 211b High Road, East Finchley … and moved into his own flat [in Montagu Square] off Baker Street.'[19]

Said Sellers' first wife Anne (to whom he was married 1954–1963), 'Peg never really let Peter go, and right up to the end of our marriage, she would ring him every single day. If there was a fog outside, she'd tell him to be careful, and if it was cold, she'd tell him to wrap up warmly.'[20]

Said Hattie Proudfoot, when Sellers' mother Peg came to visit, 'she would often do something which would annoy him so much that he used to have to get rid of her immediately. It would start in a very innocuous way.' For example, Sellers might point to the silver coffee pot and say it was 'King George II in his famous disguise', and she would laugh. Said Bryan Forbes, 'Peg would say, "I love you Peter", and he would say, "I love you Peg". "I really love you Peter." "But I really love you, Mother", and that would go on and on and build until it became a row. It was very odd to witness.'[21]

Said theatrical agent Dennis Selinger of Sellers, vis-à-vis Peg, 'He used to be quite terrible to her at times and yet probably she was the only woman in his life who really meant anything to him.'[22]

Said Michael of his paternal grandmother Peg, she 'controlled his [Sellers'] life. She may have been one person he would actually listen to. Peg would ring him and tell him he shouldn't be doing this, that, and the other, and he would at least listen and sometimes agree.'[23] According to Michael, Peg once remarked, '"My son doesn't have to think for himself. I do it for him." Her constant smothering made him feel emasculated.'[24]

Michael described Peg as 'A very claustrophobic woman. You had to hug her for half an hour every time you saw her. That was all right until she came to school to collect me. She would come and stand inside the gate and I'd say, "Can you wait in the car?", and she'd said "No", and she'd come and stand inside the gate and give me hug and say "my darling".'

'Oh God,' said Michael, as he relived this experience of being embarrassed in front of his schoolfriends.[25]

After Peg's death

Peg died on 30 January 1967, aged 72, her husband Bill having predeceased her. Peg died an alcoholic, said Anne.

Said Doris Collins, Sellers' spiritual medium and friend, 'I don't think his mother approved of all his capers and so she was a restraining influence, and when she wasn't there in the end, of course, he hadn't got anybody to restrain him, so I think that's why he used me, because he thought I could restrain him and say I was his mother, and he believed that.' Sellers saw Doris as a surrogate mother.[26]

Said Michael,

> I firmly believe that when Peg died in 1967, that finally unleashed him on an unsuspecting world. He then had absolutely no authority to answer to. After that there was nothing to hold him back. And he needed someone, because it's very easy to fall foul of your own publicity, especially when you have had an unusual and spoilt upbringing. Peg [had] always told him he was wonderful and, as an adult, everyone else was telling him he was wonderful. There was no levelling force in his life.[27]

Wherever he was, said Peter Evans, Sellers created a shrine to his mother within the house, but this did not suit his second wife Britt Ekland (to whom he was married 1964–1968). 'Finally, at the end of the marriage Britt couldn't take it anymore and she smashed this picture [of Peg], smashed it into a thousand pieces. Peter immediately fell down on his knees and started trying to put it together, weeping, weeping at this smashed photograph.'[28]

Chapter 4

Sellers Embarks on a Career

In autumn 1939, Sellers and his mother Peg moved to the seaside town of Ilfracombe, Devon, where they were reunited with Bill, who was currently employed as pianist at the town's Victorian Pavilion Theatre. Here, Peg found employment at the box office, as did Sellers himself, for he told Parkinson, 'I began as sweeper up at ten bob a week. After that I used to take tickets on the door, then I did front of house which is, as most people know, box office. From box office I went to assistant stage manager; front of house; lights; stage manager.'[1]

The Second World War commenced on 3 September 1939, following Germany's invasion of Poland 2 days earlier.

The war was almost over, said Michael, when his father, 'approaching the military call-up age of 18, volunteered for the RAF hoping to become a Spitfire pilot, but poor eyesight meant that he could never qualify.' Nonetheless, his show business background qualified him for the RAF *Gang Show*, a variety entertainment founded by actor, theatrical producer, and songwriter Ralph Reader in 1932. During the war, Reader recruited *Gang Show* members into the RAF and staged performances in order to boost the morale of the troops.

'His profession, on entering the service, was listed as an "entertainer",' Michael continued, 'a tag which led to his posting to India,' where the *Gang Show* 'was entertaining the homesick troops.'[2]

When the war was over, Sellers returned to his parents' new home in East Finchley. Secombe described how Sellers, in his youth, had played with 'some of the established dance bands'. But because life as a 'star band drummer' was very competitive, said Michael, 'instead, he devised an act as a mimic and comedian, practising for hours in front of a mirror to perfect the correct expressions.'[3] His mother Peg, however, was ambitious for him, said Michael, and in early 1946 'she persuaded a Soho agent, Dennis Selinger, to see her son. Dad stayed with Dennis [i.e., retained him as his agent] for almost twenty years.'[4]

Meanwhile, in regard to the possibility of Sellers embarking on any romantic attachments, said Graham Stark, his mother Peg 'was not obviously happy when women emerged because it was a threat to her love for him.'[5] But in 1946, despite Peg's best endeavours, Sellers became enamoured of Hilda Parkin from Norfolk, her family, like his, being in show business. Sellers wrote to Hilda over the course of three years, sometimes as many as three letters a day running into as many as sixteen pages! For example:

If you ever took it in your mind to pack me in, I would go completely round the bend. I need you so much. When I get to the top, I'll get you a Rolls Royce and throw in a few butlers for luck.

And in November 1946:

Hilda, my dearest darling. Mum woke me up this morning with a cup of tea and your lovely letter. Hilda would you marry me next year? We will both be 22.

But Sellers' entreaties were to no avail, and Hilda turned down his offer of marriage.[6]

Urged on to do so by a friend, Sellers applied for, and was accepted for, a job as comedian in a supporting role at London's Windmill Theatre. This was for a period of six weeks, commencing on 17 March 1948. Sellers subsequently featured on the weekly BBC radio variety programmes *Show Time*, and *Variety Bandbox*. He also became a resident artist on the top-rated show *Ray's A Laugh*, hosted by Ted Ray, who, said Michael, 'was distantly related to us through the vivacious Ma Ray's kinsfolk'. (This is not certain, Ted Ray's original name being Charles Olden.) In October 1949, Sellers played at the London Palladium 'in support of the charismatic Gracie Fields'.[7] It was at this time that Sellers acquired a 16mm camera. Photography was to become a lifelong passion of his.

Four comedians would now come together who became famous the world over as stars of the radio comedy programme *The Goon Show*. They were Spike Milligan, Harry Secombe, Michael Bentine, and Peter Sellers.

'Spike' Milligan

Terence Alan Milligan, who became known as 'Spike', was born on 16 April 1918 at the Military Hospital, Ahmednagar, India, where his Irish-born father Leo was serving as a sergeant major in the British Army. Leo was married to Florence (née Kettleband), who was English.

Cuts in the armed forces lead to the Milligans having to return to England. They settled in Catford, south London.

In January 1944, during the Battle of Monte Cassino in Italy, Milligan was wounded by mortar shell 'and severely shell shocked' whilst serving as signaller in the Royal Artillery. This terminated his military service.[8] As a result of this experience, he spent time in a psychiatric hospital near Sorrento, Italy.[9]

Harry Secombe

Secombe was born in Swansea, South Wales on 8 September 1921. His father Frederick was a grocer and married to Jane (née Davies). During the war he served with No. 132 Field Regiment, Royal Artillery.

Michael Bentine

Michael Bentine was born on 26 January 1922 in Watford, Hertfordshire. His father Adam, a Peruvian, was an engineer and married to Florence (née Dawkins), who was English. Bentine was educated at Eton College. During the war he served as an intelligence officer in the RAF.

How did the four Goons meet?

It was in the Officers' Club, Naples, Italy, said Milligan, that he first met Harry Secombe. 'We were playing for dancing and cabaret': Milligan being a trumpeter, and Secombe a singer and comedian.[10] The two were to remain friends.

Milligan was demobbed in May 1945, but he stayed on in Italy and toured with the 'Bill Hall Trio' in a show called *Barbary Coast*, in which 'he started to perform sketches that he had written'.[11]

Secombe met Bentine in October 1946, when both men were auditioning for a six-week show at the West End's Windmill Theatre.[12]

In New Year, 1949, Secombe performed in the radio series *Third Division*, and Bentine and Sellers joined the cast.[13]

In late 1949, Milligan went to watch Secombe perform at London's Hackney Empire theatre, and in the bar after the show, Secombe introduced Milligan 'to another up-and-coming comedian, Peter Sellers'.[14]

Said Bentine, '*The Goon Show* came about as the direct result of an evening Harry [Secombe] and I spent with Jimmy Grafton at the *Grafton Arms*. We took Spike [Milligan] to the pub to meet Jimmy, and later introduced Mine Host [Grafton] to the youthful Peter Sellers.'[15]

Said Secombe, 'Mike [Bentine] and I took Peter along to Graftons. He was so obviously one of us and his repertoire of impressions was formidable. Like the rest of us, he had been in the services and shared our lunatic sense of humour. Spike and Peter took to each other immediately and soon the four of us were meeting up regularly.'[16]

James Douglas 'Jimmy' Grafton was resident landlord of the Grafton Arms, 2 Strutton Ground, Westminster, a family owned public house. A former major in the Bedfordshire and Hertfordshire Regiment, he had participated in Operation Market Garden (September 1944, which aimed to create a bridgehead across the River Rhine and thus open the way for Allied forces to penetrate deep into Germany). For his bravery, he was awarded the Military Cross. Not only was Grafton sympathetic to budding artists, he was also artistic himself.

The Grafton Arms became the regular meeting place for the four comedians, and it was here that they honed their skills. When they performed there, 'in say mime routine', said Milligan, it used to 'keep customers out of the pub for months!'[17]

Grafton wrote scripts for comedian Derek Roy, who performed at the Grafton Arms, and in 1948 he invited Milligan to join him in writing for Roy, who was currently appearing in *Variety Bandbox*. So, Jimmy had an 'in into broadcasting', said Milligan.[18] The BBC got wind of this and asked Jimmy and Spike to write for a radio show, *Hip Hip Hoo Roy*.[19]

The Goon Show is born

Sellers 'had worked at the BBC and knew a producer, Pat Dixon', said Milligan. 'They met, and Pat asked Spike to write a script – the first *Goon Show* – but when the show first aired on 28 May 1951 it was called

The Crazy People.' The producer was Dennis Main Wilson, producer of radio and television programmes mainly for the BBC, and the shows were generally broadcast live on Sundays. At Spike's insistence, the name was 'changed to *The Goon Show* for the second series.'[20]

The last episode of *The Goon Show*, entitled 'The Last Smoking Seagoon', was broadcast in January 1960. The four 'Goons', said Bentine, 'really were like the Four Musketeers, and it is hard to feel closer to each other than that.'[21]

Max Geldray was a harmonica player whose jazz quartet provided musical interludes for *The Goon Shows*. He had first met Sellers in 1951, at a trial recording of *The Goon Show*.[22] Said Geldray of Sellers, 'He was ten years younger than me, and did ask questions and for advice but, invariably, he would do as he wanted.'[23]

In November 1952, BBC radio and television producer Peter Eton took over as producer of *The Goon Show*. There was an argument, said Secombe, 'during which Sellers threatened to leave the show. "All right", said Eton. "Bugger off then!" and Sellers, having started to leave the room, came back and sat down again.'[24] This was a humbling experience for Sellers, who, with the advent of fame and fortune, would soon be the one who called the tune!

Meanwhile, Milligan suffered several severe episodes of depression; for some of which he was hospitalised. His depression was exacerbated by the pressure of having to write scripts for *The Goon Show* on a regular basis. However, Sellers, he said, 'didn't understand mental illness'. In other words, he was lacking in empathy.

Empathy: The ability to understand and share the feelings of another.[25]

Sellers 'kept coming to the flat all the time and his phone had broken down and he wanted to use mine. And I couldn't stand the noise. I said, "Tell him to stop it". He said, "Oh, tell him not to be so silly".' Whereupon, Milligan 'got a potato knife from the kitchen'. Said he, 'I had been wanting to get into hospital and I felt, "Why won't they put me in hospital?" I thought, "If I get a knife and try and kill him, they will put me in somewhere… and I did".' The outcome was that Sellers survived and Milligan was duly admitted to hospital and put 'under deep narcosis'.[26]

Said film critic Barry Norman of Sellers, 'he was a very disturbed and egocentric man whose empathy with other people was virtually non-existent, and whose vision of the truth was whatever suited his purposes best.'[27]

Chapter 5

Wife Number One: Anne Aspinwall-Howe (Married to Sellers 1951–1963)

It was his agent Dennis Selinger who, in 1949, introduced Sellers to 'an up and coming young actress', (Charlotte) Anne Aspinwall-Howe, an Australian, who would become his wife. The meeting took place at the BBC's offices at Great Portland Place, London.[1]

Anne was born on 25 February 1930 in Java, Indonesia. She was, therefore, five years Sellers' junior. Her father Arthur, from Ilford, Essex, had married her mother Kathleen (née Miles), of Ringwood, Victoria, Australia in 1927.

Anne was not particularly bowled over with Sellers when she first met him, she said, because he was 'very fat, with long wavy hair, and he used to wear these huge suits with great wide shoulders and looked rather like a spiv'. However, when she saw him on stage, she described him as 'absolutely extraordinary, wonderful'.[2]

Sellers and Anne were married at Caxton Hall, Westminster on 15 September 1951. However, said Michael, his parents Peg and Bill, 'refused to attend the wedding and she [Peg] devised all sorts of devious schemes to wreck the marriage. She wanted her son back at all costs.'[3] The couple moved into 'a penthouse with lovely views over Hyde Park'. They subsequently relocated to a rented flat in Highgate, and then to a three-bedroomed property in Muswell Hill, which was their first home of their own.[4]

By this time, said Michael, Sellers had become obsessed with photography. He was 'spending money ridiculously and was making no provision for income tax or any other emergency.'[5] Meanwhile, in summer 1952, at the end of Series Two, Bentine left *The Goon Show*. The reason was, said Michael, that 'he and Spike no longer saw eye to eye'.[6]

Before long, cracks in the marriage began to appear. Seller's 'primary objective at this time', said Michael, 'was to persuade my mother to abandon her career. His reasons were totally selfish. He could not bear to think of my mother being involved in any other way of life that did not include him.'[7] Said Anne,

> he was never very happy with me acting. He preferred me to be around the whole time. He never really liked me going away anywhere. In fact, he was always throwing tantrums or saying he won't let me out of the flat; or he's taken a hundred aspirins just as I was going on stage. He was like a spoilt child really. However badly he had behaved as a child, he was allowed to get away with it, and I guess he thought, well, that was instinctive of him, he thought that all women would be like his mother.[8]

Their son was born on 2 April 1954 and christened Michael Peter Anthony Sellers. As a result of this happy event, said Michael, there was a reconciliation between his grandmother Peg and Sellers' wife Anne.[9]

On 15 July 1956 the family relocated to 83 Oakleigh Avenue, Whetstone, in the North London suburb of Barnet. Anne described it as 'a nice suburban house', and Sellers nicknamed it 'St Fred's'. On 16 October 1957, their daughter Sarah Jane was born.

In 1960, said Michael, Sellers saw a house 'advertised in the *Sunday Times* and decided he had to have that'.[10] This was the Manor House, Chipperfield, near King's Langley, Hertfordshire. Having viewed the property with Anne, he duly purchased it. The Elizabethan manor house, said Michael, lay 'in the heart of the English countryside. We had our own tennis courts and swimming pool, while two Tudor tithe barns stood in the paddocks.'[11]

So, from 'St Fred's' at Whetstone, said Anne, they moved into

> this huge mansion. We had a butler and a cook and God knows what. I'll really never know what we were doing there. I'm not sure that Peter ever knew what we were doing there either. We had a whole wing where he had a dark room and a little cinema and that was where he cut his films. He liked the whole process from beginning to end.

'We did move a lot,' said Anne. 'I'm not quite sure why. I guess he got sick of wherever we were.' Anne could count up to probably eight different houses, 'But he would get fed up with one, or it wasn't big enough or something.'[12]

A decade or so later, Sellers, with a broad smile on his face, described his peripatetic lifestyle. 'The great thing about this business of being an actor is that you lead the life of a gypsy. You don't have to stay in any one place too long'.

Did that suit him?

> Very much, yes. I've been brought up with it. I come from a theatrical family. I've been touring round all my life. I like roots. Every actor, of course, every person has roots: especially actors, because usually they live in dressing rooms and in digs and skips; baskets you know. So, to have roots is a big thing, but I mean at the same time you mustn't let them hang round your neck.[13]

'Peter was always extremely inconsistent,' said Anne, 'always looking for something new. This applied not only to his professional life but also to his private life. He loved new toys, new cars, new characters – new wives too. But the fascination soon wore off. He was like a child. He never really grew up, and it made him very difficult to live with.'[14]

It was whilst they were living at Chipperfield Manor, said Anne, that Sellers became an international star. But 'the bad times really started when we moved into that house'.

Meanwhile, trouble was brewing. Said Michael,

> the problems for Peter Sellers the man, really began when he became a superstar. Suddenly, there were people running around after him, nothing was too difficult for him. For a man lacking in self-control, it was a dangerous position to be in. On a film set he was given too much power and control and would throw tantrums. Sometimes he wouldn't appear for a scene.[15]

When Sellers became famous, said Michael 'he didn't exactly ditch his old friends, he just saw less of them. Suddenly, he was a big star out in Hollywood, losing sight of what he really was and where he had come from.'[16]

Said Anne, 'Every character he played he would bring home. It was very unnerving. He'd come home as an Indian doctor or some little Welsh man; bit like living on the edge of a precipice; you weren't quite sure whether he'd be absolutely wonderful, or absolutely ghastly, and we'd have some sort of terrible row.' There were endless rows between his parents, said Michael.[17]

One day, when his father returned home from work, said Michael, and his mother Anne was reading her book, Sellers shouted

> 'What the bloody hell is the matter with you? Why are you so miserable?' All hell was let loose. Dad grabbed a vase and threw it straight at her. It missed her by an inch or two and smashed against the wall. Unable to control his anger he went through to the bathroom, tore a towel rail from the floor and twisted its tubular steel like a piece of rubber piping. Next, he destroyed a set of pictures that hung in the dressing room and tore every coat hook from the wall. One night he emptied a bottle of milk over her.[18]

On another occasion, after a party,

> it transpired that Mum had too many compliments paid to her, which upset Dad. When they got home, he tore my mother's dress from her and in the morning when I went through into their bedroom it was lying on the floor in shreds.[19]

Dad sought an impossible commitment from her; my mother felt she lived in a gilded cage. As long as she was in the house, and giving him her undivided attention, then Dad would be content. If he was working in the studios, he would ring three or four times a day to check her movements. If she left the house even to go shopping, she would be subjected to interrogation.

We woke one morning to find that the entire lounge had been devastated, the debris scattered everywhere. This was retribution for Mum saying she wanted to leave home. Like a man suffering from 'diminished responsibility', Dad had run amok. Beautiful *objets d'art*, caringly and lovingly collected through their marriage, were now lying on the floor in many hundreds of broken pieces. When I saw Mum, she looked like a ghost and had bruises all over her. I started to cry. In later years I learnt that Dad had threatened to kill her that night.[20]

For Sellers, even family holidays were a problem. Said Michael, 'it was difficult for him to gloss over the fact that holidays bored him. It was not unknown for him to abandon us completely and return to London as soon as he became disenchanted.'[21]

The filming of *The Millionairess* (1960), which was set in London, put a further strain on the marriage. In the film, Sellers was cast as Dr Kabir and Italian film actress and singer Sophia Loren, as Epifania. (Sophia Loren was at that time married to Italian film producer, Carlo Ponti.) Said Michael, when he was playing the leading man opposite Sophia Loren, 'Dad bloomed with sudden happiness, like the onrush of spring.'[22] He even went so far as to tell his wife 'that I've fallen madly in love with Sophia Loren'.

Said Anne of her husband, he

> was cast opposite this stunningly beautiful woman, which she was and still is. He just got totally carried away with it and he became besotted by her. I'm not sure if this was returned but he felt it was, and it was very genuine for him. He then treated me as his mother, that I should allow him to do whatever he wanted to do, and he would come to me with his problems about Sophia. Things got very difficult.

In the film, Epifania (Sophia) asks Dr Kabir (Sellers), 'Are you married?' to which he replies, 'To science, science is my bride.' Whereupon, she says, 'Take another wife. I wouldn't be jealous of her. I want to marry you.' For someone as emotionally unstable as Sellers, to stare into the eyes of such a beautiful woman with those words issuing from her lips was a sure-fire recipe for disaster. 'He became besotted by her,' said his wife Anne.[23]

Michael 'took an instant dislike to Sophia Loren'. Why? 'I'd say in hindsight it was because of the ructions she was causing in the family,' he said. Home movies show Michael as a jolly, amiable little boy who almost invariably had a smile on his face. But even at the tender age of 6, he realised that his father's infatuation with Sophia was not only hurtful for his mother Anne, but also threatened his own harmonious little world.

Said Milligan of Sellers and Sophia, 'I think there was an invisible continuum between them, and if the chance presented itself, he might have gone for her hook, line, and sinker.'[24]

Said Michael, 'One night, Dad woke up and gripped Mum's arm as if the privacy of their bedroom had been invaded. "Shush, don't say anything," Dad motioned. "I can feel her presence coming into the room. Yes, she is here with us." "Who is?" "It's Sophia … Sophia," Dad whispered.'[25] Early one morning at 3 a.m. Michael was 'hauled' from his bed and asked, 'Do you think I should divorce your mummy?'[26]

When Sellers purchased a flat in Hampstead, he asked South African architect Ted Levy to 'design the fabric of the entire penthouse'. But when the family moved in, Sellers told Levy to take his wife Anne, away. '"I don't want her," he yelled at him.' But when Anne told Sellers that she had decided to leave home, 'he burst into tears and threatened to jump from the penthouse balcony. It was not the first time he had spoken of suicide. This was always his crutch in a crisis.'[27] Sellers subsequently 'grabbed hold of Mother and started to strangle her,' and as a result, 'Mum was badly bruised and had to wear long-sleeved dresses for days in order to cover her injuries. She knew now that she would have to leave home to escape his tyranny.'[28]

When Sellers lured Anne back to the penthouse by way of a ruse, said Michael (she was now living at her widowed mother Kathleen's house, in Bovingdon Green, Hertfordshire), Sellers 'whirled round and slammed the door behind them. "Now try and leave. You're never going to get out," he cried, locking the door.'[29]

Meanwhile, in October 1962, Sellers' father Bill died at the age of 62. Anne summed up the situation as follows:

He never wanted to split up: he didn't want a divorce. He never wanted to leave. He wanted to be able to do what he liked wherever he liked, and come back and tell 'Mamma' [i.e., Anne herself] what was going on, and I was supposed to be sympathetic to him. It didn't actually work, so eventually, I guess I left.[30]

Sellers and Anne were divorced on 7 March 1963, Sellers having finally agreed that the divorce should go ahead. Whereupon he 'bought a lovely little cottage back in Hampstead' for Anne. 'It was in Golden Yard – only a mile away from the penthouse.'[31] In October 1963, Anne married Ted Levy, and in that same year, Michael, now aged 9, commenced at boarding school.

Sellers attended their daughter Sarah's sixth birthday party, soon after Anne had remarried. And now that the marriage was over, said Bert Mortimer, Sellers became very depressed; and 'there were times when I genuinely thought that he would commit suicide. He was there on his own. So that's when I moved in.' Also, 'Mr and Mrs [Bryan] Forbes used to come up quite a lot and hold his hand till he went to sleep.'[32]

She and Peter were together for about fifteen years, said Anne, 'but finally I went through a period of actually hating him'.[33] However,

> Although it was quite bitter for a time, when we split, we ended up actually remaining good friends. He used to introduce me to all his new acquisitions in the way of girlfriends, so that 'Mum' could see them and tell him what I thought of them. A strange man.[34] I would think I have probably laughed more with him than anybody I have known in my life. And probably cried more too.[35]

Chapter 6

Wife Number Two: Britt Ekland (Married to Sellers 1964–1968)

Britt described how she met Sellers on 8 February 1964 while she was involved in a photo shoot at the Dorchester Hotel, London.[1]

Sellers had noticed Britt's photograph on the front page of the *Evening News*. 'She had just arrived in England and I thought what I saw was very good, and I thought that I would like to meet what I saw.' And then, to his surprise, he learnt that Britt was staying at the same hotel.[2] But, whereas he occupied the Dorchester's luxurious 'Oliver Messel' suite, said Britt, 'I was in a cupboard!'[3]

Sellers 'sent his valet over', continued Britt. He told her, 'Mr Sellers would like to invite you for a drink.' All she knew about him was that he had been a judge on a 'Miss Universe' contest. 'I didn't know who he was. I didn't know that he was an actor.' He then drove her to the Odeon Theatre, Leicester Square to see him starring in the film *The Pink Panther*! 'I see the movie and of course, now I know who he is!'[4]

Said Sellers, 'I took lots of pictures of her [i.e., photographs], and when she went away I missed her terribly, and I thought "this was it".'[5] Eleven days later, on 19 February 1964, they were married.[6] Two months prior to Sellers proposing to Britt, said Michael, 'Maurice Woodruff, a clairvoyant he regularly consulted, had told Dad that he would marry a girl with the initials "B.E."'[7]

Britt was born on 6 October 1942. She was therefore seventeen years Sellers' junior. 'I was very young when I married Peter Sellers,' she said, 'and I was very naive and very unsophisticated. I had just come out of Sweden. I could speak English because we were taught in school.'[8]

On 15 March 1964, Sellers wrote to Britt from California as follows:

I have a dreadful fear at the back of my mind that you might leave me. I love you so desperately, and think you are so absolutely wonderful in every way, that I find it very difficult to understand why you married me. You who are just the most lovely thing in the whole world. What do you see in me? I'm not handsome. I'm not tall. I'm not special in any way.

He confessed to Britt that he felt 'quite faint and ill and terrible and wretched and awful' at the thought that she might be unfaithful to him. 'Without any doubt, I am a raving idiot and I ought to have my head examined.'[9]

This letter, which came to light in 2009, is important because it reveals Sellers as a desperately insecure person and also a very self-deprecating one.

The couple set up home at Brookfield, Elstead, Surrey: a property that Sellers had acquired the previous year. This was a fifteenth-century manor house with a lake and extensive grounds.

In respect of her relationship with Sellers, Britt said, 'I was really his little toy. He decided my life. I was offered lots of films – and if he didn't like it, he would just say, no she's not going to do that. So, he decided all aspects of my life.' But, 'I was easy going and I was young.'[10]

Said Bert Mortimer, 'I was very, very happy for him. I've never seen him so happy, I'd only been with him a couple of years, but he had a good lady on his arm and as far as I could see she genuinely loved him, and I thought "Oh, great!" and this made life a lot easier for everybody around him.'[11]

Sure enough, in a film clip, Britt is to be seen with both arms around Sellers' neck and he is smiling broadly. However, said Michael, 'His love, as always, had to be conveyed with extravagant presents and he also bestowed on Britt a black-diamond mink coat: a diamond-studded gold brooch, a sports car – and a Dachshund she named "Pepe".' This was in addition to an antique Victorian engagement ring 'of emeralds, diamonds, and rubies'.[12]

On 20 March 1964, during a visit to the USA, Sellers recorded an interview with Steve Allen, to be aired shortly afterwards on US television's *Steve Allen Show*. In regard to his wife, he said, 'I call Britt my Britt you see, because she belongs to me.' This is clearly a reflection of how he felt about her, i.e. as a possession.[13]

In April 1964, said Michael, his father was admitted to the Cedars of Lebanon Hospital, Los Angeles, where, on 5 April, he 'suffered seven consecutive heart attacks'.[14] Sellers himself put the figure at 'thirteen heart attacks in a row'.[15] This was only forty-six days after his marriage to Britt.

When Britt fell pregnant in spring 1964, said Michael, Sellers said that 'he was urging her to have an abortion. "I've got Michael, I've got Sarah. I don't want any more children." When he told Mum [Anne], she was appalled.'[16]

Meanwhile, US publisher and founder of *Playboy* Hugh Hefner had asked Sellers if he would take some photographs of Britt in the nude for a magazine. Said she, 'I said to Peter, "I have never, never in my life posed for nude photographs"; but he would not listen to me. There was nothing that I could say or do. I knew that this was not normal. I knew that this was not how a normal man should behave towards his wife, particularly when she's pregnant.' But 'If you are a genius, it's a licence to behave badly,' she said ruefully.[17] On 20 January 1965 their daughter Victoria was born at the Welbeck Street Clinic, London.[18]

Further evidence of Sellers' controlling nature soon became apparent. 'Dad was desperately jealous of Britt,' said Michael. 'He felt that a younger and more handsome man might make a play for her and that she would be especially vulnerable on a film set without him. Whenever Britt was offered a movie, the script would be carefully scrutinised by Dad, who would then do everything in his power to talk Britt out of accepting the part.'

Said Roger Lewis of Sellers and Britt, 'he was convinced that he would lose her because he didn't really believe that anyone like her would want to be with him. He was obsessed that she was being seduced by her other co-stars here, there, and everywhere. He was mad with jealousy.'[19]

'There was only one way to appease Britt,' Michael continued, 'while ensuring that he was able to keep a protective eye on her, and that was to become a husband and wife team and work on movies together.' This was subsequently the case with *After the Fox* (1966) and *The Bobo* (1967).[20] However, during the filming of *After the Fox*, Sellers screamed at Britt '"You're a lousy bloody actress" and threw a chair at her.'[21]

Meanwhile, said Michael, as a result of the family constantly moving house, by the time he was aged 12 he had attended nine different schools.

During the filming of *The Bobo*, Sellers instructed his solicitors 'to write to Britt and tell her that he intended to file for divorce'. The following day, he changed his mind, 'and repaired his rift with Britt with a profusion of kisses and the usual gifts.' However, 'during their next serious row' he stamped on the gold Cartier watch he had given her and threw 'the particles down the loo'.[22]

When Sellers visited Genoa, he purchased a brand-new yacht costing £150,000, which he named *The Bobo*, after the film. It had a crew of three. However, 'in time, the enjoyment of being aboard *The Bobo* began to wane,' said Michael.[23]

Sellers and Britt were in Rome when news came that Sellers' mother Peg was ill, and shortly afterwards, on 30 January 1967, she died. When he finally left Rome, said Michael, 'it was too late. He was filled with remorse and for weeks after the funeral he was deeply depressed.' On their return home, 'Dad did something very strange'. He 'brought Peg's clothes from her apartment and burnt them in a pile in the garden incinerator.' However, subsequently 'he would light a candle to her memory every Friday.'[24]

During another row, during which Sellers and Britt slapped each other's faces, Britt accidentally knocked a framed picture of Peg off the dresser in the living room. 'It crashed to the floor and seeing it all in shattered pieces, Dad burst into tears, sobbing that Britt had ruined his favourite picture of Peg,' said Michael. This was on 6 February 1967, which was the day before he was presented with the CBE (Commander of the Most Excellent Order of the British Empire) by Her Majesty the Queen at Buckingham Palace.[25]

In the summer of 1968, Sellers told his children that he intended to divorce Britt. 'I wouldn't advise either of you ever to get married. Marriage simply doesn't work,' he said. Britt was duly granted a divorce on 18 December 1968, on the grounds of mental cruelty, 'along with a £30,000 settlement'. She was also 'given care and control of Victoria with joint custody'.[26]

Subsequently, after an evening dinner party with Britt and some friends, said Michael, 'Dad was feeling morose and did not seem to understand why or how their divorce had come about. Just as Victoria was going to bed in the Clarges Street flat [in Mayfair, which Sellers had given Britt the use of], he suddenly threatened to kill Britt' by pointing a double-barrelled shotgun at her. However, Britt talked him out of it. 'Dad crumpled on the sofa and burst into tears like a child, burying his head between his hands,' said Michael. When Britt subsequently fell in love with Italian producer Count Ascanio Cicogna, known as 'Bino', Sellers 'threatened to have Victoria made a ward of court if Britt lived with Bino. He hired a private eye to spy on them.'[27]

Appearing on BBC Radio 4's programme *Desert Island Discs* in 1994, Britt stated that she had really loved Sellers and that she had done her best in the marriage.[28] 'Dad's breed of women didn't appeal to me very much,' said Michael, but he confessed to having had a warm relationship with Britt. She was 'the exception and I formed a closer attachment to her than any of the others.'[29] In fact, Britt was only twelve years his senior.

In 1973, Britt had a son, Nic, by US record producer Lou Adler. In 1984, Britt married James McDonnell (stage name Slim Jim Phantom), drummer for the US band Stray Cats. She bore him a son, Thomas. They divorced in 1992.

Chapter 7

Wife Number Three: Miranda Quarry (Married to Sellers 1970–1974)

Sellers married Miranda Quarry (née MacMillan) at Caxton Hall, London on 24 August 1970. Born on 27 May 1947, she was therefore twenty-one years Sellers' junior.

Miranda was the stepdaughter of Lord Mancroft, former Conservative Cabinet Minister and Chairman of the Cunard shipping and cruise line company. The couple set up home in Cheyne Gardens, Chelsea.

Lord and Lady Mancroft objected to the marriage on the grounds that Sellers was significantly older than their daughter Miranda and also that he was an entertainer with a working-class background. 'Fame was not a substitute for blue-blooded breeding,' said Michael. 'They wanted Miranda to marry into the aristocracy, preferably someone with a title.'[1]

Best man at the wedding was Bert Mortimer. He described how, when he was with Sellers and Miranda on their yacht in the South of France during their honeymoon, suddenly, 'one morning, we couldn't find him. And then the ship-to-shore phone rang and it was him. He'd booked himself into a hotel, left his bride on the yacht, and we couldn't work out why. And I think he regretted it almost immediately. It wasn't working out, it wasn't him.'[2]

In March 1971, the couple relocated to Ireland, Sellers having purchased Carton House, set in 1,000 acres of parkland. The estate was close to the village of Maynooth, in County Kildare, and 'just over an hour's run from Dublin'. His career had 'hit a very rough patch', said Michael, and he therefore sold his yacht *The Bobo*, his Clarges Street apartment, and all his motor cars, apart from the Mercedes which he had bought second-hand from Blake Edwards. 'It was Blake who had a hand in determining our move from London to Ireland. The Republic was a tax haven for writers and artists who were classified as "exempt".'[3]

As was the case with Sellers' previous two wives, tensions soon became evident. As time went by, said Michael 'the animosity and rows grew more fearful'. For example, Sellers 'seized the wedding album in a rage … and began tearing up their wedding pictures. "That was the most terrible day of my life," he ranted. "Why did I marry her?"' He then instructed Bert Mortimer to throw all of Miranda's jewellery into the lake, which Bert had the good sense not to do.[4]

When a stranger telephoned the house 'and asked for Miranda', Sellers demanded to know who it was. 'I want proof of your innocence,' he raged at Miranda and he proceeded to 'bug' the telephone in order that he could listen to her calls.[5]

Michael described how, when his father and Miranda 'were out in his silver Rolls-Royce', Sellers 'became so incensed' by something she said, 'that he deliberately crashed the car. He drove into another Rolls and then reversed into the car behind.'[6]

Miranda possessed five dogs and two cats, which she called her 'babies'.[7] In a scene which could easily have come from a *Pink Panther* film, Sellers was driven to distraction by the squawking of Miranda's ten parrots, and 'unable to quieten the cockatoo, attempted to strangle it, but the bird's flapping wings prevented him from tightening his grip on its neck.' However, said Michael, the following morning, the bird was discovered 'lying dead in her cage. Dad wore an expression of guilt.'[8]

In autumn 1972, twelve years after the final episode of *The Goon Show* had aired on BBC radio, said Secombe, the Goons were 'summoned back to record a special show as part of the BBC Silver Jubilee celebrations.' This was transmitted on 5 October from Camden Theatre. Guests included Prince Philip, Princess Margaret, Lord Snowdon, and Princess Anne. Also in attendance were Max Geldray and singer, drummer, and band leader Ray Ellington (who also provided musical interludes for *The Goon Show*). Prince Charles 'was unable to attend' and sent his apologies.[9]

'Slowly but surely, Dad began to tire of Ireland,' said Michael, 'but he tired more of the long round of social parties that Miranda inveigled him into attending. He began to admit that he didn't like her friends: he labelled them as "prize bores". Dad yearned to get back to England and to meet up again with his old friends. He liked to see Spike, David and Graham,' i.e. Milligan, Lodge, and Stark respectively.[10] Actor David

Lodge had first met Sellers in early 1945, as a fellow performer in the RAF *Gang Show*.

The outcome was that in late 1972, Sellers left Ireland and returned to London, where he rented a property in Eaton Mews.[11] Meanwhile, Miranda relocated to a house in Wiltshire which the couple owned jointly. A legal separation was agreed, whereupon, said Michael, 'Dad talked about ending his life, but I told him not to talk in such a way.'[12]

Christina Wachtmeister (known to her friends as 'Titi'), daughter of the Swedish Ambassador to the USA, was Sellers' lady friend from 1972 to 1975. Said she to Michael, 'How can I begin to understand him?' 'I laughed at her naivety,' Michael said. 'It would be impossible to begin to answer that question. It would need a seminar to attempt to explain Dad's complexities.'[13] The relationship ended when 'a handsome young Cypriot started casting Titi admiring glances', when the couple were on holiday in Cyprus.[14] Whereupon, Sellers threw Titi's suitcase through the door of the restaurant 'like a caber. It crashed onto a table, shattering wine bottles, glasses and crockery'. But unfortunately it was not Titi's table, but that of a complete stranger![15]

When Sellers' relationship with 'Titi' Wachtmeister was over, said Michael, 'Once more he was overcome with loneliness and depression and would call us on any pretext, engaging us in long conversations. Often, he would complain that we didn't see him enough, that we were disloyal and uncaring.'[16]

Meanwhile, in 1973, Sellers fell in love with US actress and singer Liza Minnelli. When she subsequently broke off the affair, said Michael, 'he poured out his heart to me as though our roles as father and son were reversed. "I loved her, Mike. I really did", he whispered, "and I love her now … that's why it hurts so much". I remember tears coming into his eyes.'[17] As Michael, now aged 19, drove his father home through the streets of London at four o'clock in the morning, he remarked 'it was cold and Dad turned up the collar of his coat, his shoulders hunched with the dejection of a man burdened with all the troubles of the world.'[18] It has to be said that whereas Michael was generally kind, considerate, and supportive towards his father, such loving gestures were not always reciprocated by Sellers in respect of his children: quite the reverse, in fact.

On 27 September 1974, Sellers and Miranda were divorced.

Miranda was subsequently married to Sir Nicolas Nuttall (from 1975 to 1983), and to the 2nd Earl of Stockton (from 1995 to 2011).

Chapter 8

Ambition: Talent: Humility

Ambition

Sellers was always ambitious, even in his later years. In 1970, for the BBC cinema review programme *Film Night*, he declared, 'I'm a very ambitious person. I don't believe by any means, that I've even begun to do what's inside me. I have a burning fire inside me to do certain things which I know I'm going to do, and I'm going to defeat all these berks that are around me and I'm going to do it.'[1]

In 1971, Sellers read Jerzy Kosinski's novel, *Being There*. Said he, my

> great, great, great, ambition is to do something as an actor which I will leave behind me, because I know I have it in me, and no sod is going to kill it in the future, because whatever I have, it may be nothing, but whatever I have, I'm going to put up there, so long as I can get work, that is, and do it. That's the way I feel about it right now any way.[2]

This became an obsession. 'That was his one plan, to get this off the ground,' said Bert Mortimer.[3] But it would take Sellers almost a decade to fulfil his ambition.

Talent

Sellers was a master impersonator, and his grasp of different accents was utterly amazing. For example, in a single clip he could switch from 'posh London' to 'Cockney London', Cornish, Glaswegian, Edinburgh, American, and finish up by taking off the rich, Hampshire accent of the late cricket commentator, John Arlott! And when parody was added to the mix, the results were spectacular and hilarious.

> Parody: imitation for comic effect.[4]

Angela Morley was musical director of *The Goon Show* from 1952 onwards. If, for some reason, Sellers could not attend a rehearsal, she said, then because 'he did so many voices ... they had to bring in about four people to replace him!'[5]

Said comedy actor Roy Hudd, of Sellers, 'It is impossible to explain his mastery. All sorts of idiosyncrasies of speech, movement and appearance were stored away in his memory to be brought out when he had to create a character.'[6]

Sellers had used his gift of mimicry to good effect early on in his career, when he telephoned the BBC and asked to speak to Roy Speer, a senior producer. But unbeknown to Speer, Sellers was using the voice of comedian and star of BBC radio, Kenneth Horne. 'Horne' (a.k.a. Sellers) now proceeded to ask Speer to put in a good word for 'an amazing young fellow called Peter Sellers', saying, 'I think it would probably be very good if you had him on the show.' (This was in respect of a new show called *Show Time*, compèred by Australian-born comedian and actor Dick Bentley.) Finally, however, Sellers confessed to Speer. 'It's me, Peter Sellers talking. This is the only way I could get you, and would you give me a date on your show?' Whereupon, Speer called him a 'cheeky young sod', and asked him what he did. Whereupon, Sellers replied wittily, 'Well, I obviously do impersonations!'[7] The ruse was successful!

Said theatre, opera, and film director Peter Hall (who was knighted in 1977), and who directed Sellers in the stage play *Brouhaha* in 1958, 'Peter, in some respects, was as good an actor as Alec Guinness, or as good an actor as Laurence Olivier.' However, when he was acting, said Hall, 'I'm sure the play or the film was only about *him* in *his* view. It is no good arguing with that; that's the nature of that kind of psyche.'[8]

Sellers, however, was a comedic actor first and last, and when asked if he could play either 'a perfectly straight hero or a romantic part' he replied in the negative, 'we'll leave that to the young, handsome brigade. It wouldn't work.'[9] (Straight meaning serious, as opposed to comic.)[10]

Humility

Even when he became wealthy and famous, Sellers remained essentially a humble man. Referring, presumably to his films, he declared, 'I don't think I've ever seen anything of my own yet that I have ever been satisfied with.'[11]

Chapter 9

Getting into the Mindset of His Characters

In an interview by satellite link with Australian television in 1980 (which was the year of his death), Sellers was as always immaculately dressed in suit, collar and tie, but on this occasion, he was unusually serious-looking and restrained.[1] He described the trouble he had gone to in order to portray the character 'Chance', in the film *Being There*. He had his hair cut short and deliberately put on weight. It was like 'carrying a couple of heavy suitcases around with you' he said, but this was the sort of sacrifice he was prepared to make for his art.[2] However, his technique was first to master the voice of the character, before adopting the make-up and dress. Whereas for most actors, he said, it was the other way round.[3]

Sellers looked at fellow performers with a critical eye. For example, in regard to certain British crooners, he said they would begin by imitating a US accent, but then lapse into, say, a Cockney accent at the end of the song, having forgotten who they were pretending to be!

> Crooner: a singer, typically a male one, who sings sentimental songs in a soft, low voice.[4]

When he appeared on *The Mike Yarwood Show*, hosted by impressionist and comedian Mike Yarwood (which ran from 1982 to 1987), Sellers declared with that wonderful, slightly lopsided smile of his,

> I always will like the memory of playing Inspector Clouseau. Clouseau is a special sort of character. There are people like Clouseau around all over the world. He's the sort of man with great inbuilt dignity. He's an idiot and he knows that. But he wouldn't let anyone else know that. So that if something goes wrong: he falls over or something awful happens; if there's a phone call and he's told, 'There's a phone call for you, Inspector,' he says 'Ah, that will be for me,' because he wants to be one up all the time you see. There's an awful lot of people like that about.[5]

Said Dennis Main Wilson, 'He had the ability to identify completely with another person, to think his way physically and mentally and emotionally into their skin. Where did that come from? I have no idea. Is it a curse? Often.'[6]

Sellers gave the following clue as to the secret of his success. 'As soon as I can get hold of something, a character or a voice or something, I can then use that as a shield, get within it and hopefully use the character as a medium if you like, and he can come out through me.'[7] When asked if there was a 'psychic aspect' to his acting, Sellers replied, 'I think you can sometimes be inhabited by the spirit of someone who lived at some time, and maybe they come and use you as a chance to relive again.'[8] Sellers' attitude to spiritualism will be discussed shortly.

Lolita (in which Sellers played the part of playwright Clare Quilty) was filmed in the UK in 1962. Stanley Kubrick, the film's American director, said of Sellers, 'He was the only actor that I knew who had the ability to improvise. After a time, even when he wasn't on form, he fell into the spirit of the character and just took off. It was miraculous.'[9]

When asked if he made a conscious effort to 'submerge' his personality when he took on a new film character, Sellers replied, 'Oh yes, completely.'[10] However, he said, 'To see me as a character on a screen as myself would be one the dullest things you could ever experience.'[11]

Chapter 10

Sellers' Wonderful Sense of Humour

Sellers called his house at Whetstone 'St Fred's, when he could easily have given it a far grander title. In one of his home movies, he begins by saying, 'Following my dramatic success at the Workmen's Institute Penge...' It was such commonplace touches as these that endeared him to his audiences. There were similar touches in *Songs for Swingin' Sellers* and *The Best of Sellers*. For example, in 'Puttin' on the Smile', the barely articulate Lenny Goonigan begins by saying, 'Anyone got a fag?' When asked if he has ever visited 'The Deep South' (i.e. of the USA), Goonigan replies, 'I've been all over, man. You see, I've been to Brighton, Portsmouth, Truro, Penzance. I've been all over.' Similarly, in *The Goon Show*, for example, where Hercules Grytpype-Thynne (Sellers) extolls the virtues of the greatest pyramid in the world, Neddy Seagoon (Secombe) asks 'How much?' and Sellers replies 'eight bob'. Sellers did not write these scripts, but only someone such as himself and his fellow Goons with a great sense of humour could have portrayed such characters to such dazzling effect.

Film footage exists of Sellers and his mother Peg, reliving with light-hearted banter the time when she made her living by selling antiques. She purchases such items, she says, and then sells them 'at a very heavy price'. Sellers introduces his mother as 'the well-known antique dealer and candle maker. There may be some Georgian coffee still in it,' he quips, as she examines an antique silver coffee pot. Says she, 'Of course, I'm not an expert,' as she holds up the pot. Whereupon, Sellers says, 'Oh I thought you *were* an expert'.[1]

Fellow actor Ian Carmichael described how, during breaks in the filming of *I'm All Right Jack* (1959), Sellers would invite the cast round to his house where, 'He would entertain us,' by singing and playing his ukulele, and having recorded the song, 'play it back at the wrong speed. This was terribly childish, but it absolutely fascinated him, and he roared with laughter.'[2]

Sellers described how, when they were filming *The Party* (1968), in which he played bumbling Indian film star Hrundi V. Bakshi, he had to break off from the studio and drive round Hollywood for an hour or so in an effort to stop giggling uncontrollably, and compose himself.[3]

Chapter 11

The Real Peter Sellers

Despite Sellers' protestations to the contrary, there *was* a 'real' Peter Sellers, who existed in his own right, and not solely vicariously as one of his film characters. He hinted at this, when interviewed in 1972: 'Among my own intimate friends, obviously one opens up and we swap ideas and things,' he said.[1]

A hobby of Sellers' was photography, and in his time he possessed a number of superb cameras, including cine, with which he recorded his family and friends. One of these recordings begins with Sellers clowning about with fellow 'Goons' Harry Secombe and Spike Milligan, looking radiantly happy. Another clip shows him with his arm round Milligan, giving him a hug and whispering in his ear, and then turning to face the camera with that typical, rather cheeky smile on his face.[2] This is not the Sellers which one is accustomed to seeing on television or at the cinema, for these films were only intended by him for private viewings.

For example, we see Sellers cuddling a Siamese cat, whilst his mother Peg kisses it at the same time. He gives his toddler children piggybacks; rocks his daughter Sarah on the garden swing, and tenderly restores her to her feet when she falls over.[3] As his son Michael peddles along in his toy car, a US Jeep, Sellers calls out to him in a 'Bluebottle type' voice 'Michael, Michael come here at once, you naughty little boy.' Whereupon Michael, attired in his dungarees, hastily vacates the car and runs towards his mother, Anne. We see Michael climbing into various motorcars owned by his father and clambering about.[4]

Sellers 'had a 16-mm camera with live sound,' said Michael, and his children 'were supposed to perform,' whilst he gave the instructions including whether they ought to smile or not. But the viewer may have wondered whether this was for *his own* amusement rather than for *theirs*.[5] Nonetheless, the films portray Sellers as a family man, and a father who was devoted to his children.

When he added the soundtrack to these films, Sellers put on a different voice to his own. For example, he films Michael as a toddler being shown round the garden by the gardener, who talks to him in a West Country accent. So cleverly is the film dubbed that it is only when Michael, as an adult, pointed it out that we realised that the voice of the gardener is actually that of Sellers himself![6]

'Dad could be kind, gentle, caring and considerate,' said Michael.

He could fill us with joy and laughter, as he might an audience. But when the horizons clouded, and the horrific black depressive moods descended abruptly upon him, he could snarl like a tortured animal, haunted by suspicion and trapped by a persecution mania, convinced that the world, and his family, were set against him. Every member of the household, at one stage or another, experienced the bitter-sweet extremes of Dad's psychotic nature.[7]

Psychosis: a mental disorder in which thought and emotions are so impaired that perception of external reality is severely affected.[8]

'The tragedy was that he did not know how to communicate with us, or how to express his love,' said Michael.[9]

During our infancy, Dad smothered us with cuddly toys and presents; buying them in bulk from Harrods or Hamleys and spreading them all over the house. Dad felt that this was the surest method of conveying his love to us.[10]

It didn't need any one to remind us that Dad was a genius; a man whose brilliant wit and extraordinary talent would always hold a unique place in cinematographic history. But there was a penalty incurred for his genius and we, as a family, duly paid it, absorbing like a buffer the whims and insanities of his incredibly complex character which could change faster than the colours of the chameleon, and with lethal effect.[11]

Sellers bought himself a red Bentley 'Continental' motor car, and when its paintwork was chipped by flying grit he was greatly distressed. 'Feeling sorry for him, I set out to repair the car with a tin of touch-up paint I knew to be in his garage toolbox,' said Michael. But when Sellers saw what he had done, 'hauling me up to my bedroom he yanked down my trousers and whipped me with his leather belt. Mum attempted to intervene as I screamed with pain, but she was thrown aside, my father's temper, once lost, being utterly uncontrollable.'[12]

Said Hattie Proudfoot, his personal secretary, Sellers used to 'desperately look forward to seeing his children', and 'longed for them to come'. And when Michael and Sarah visited him at his Hampstead flat (following Sellers' separation from their mother Anne and their subsequent divorce in March 1963), 'he would shower them with gifts and affection. But when they arrived, he would deliberately provoke an argument with them. Perhaps Michael would say something that Peter didn't want to hear, and then he would ask that the children be taken away somewhere until the following day, and this was just so unfair on a child.'[13]

Michael, who was approaching his tenth birthday, became irritated because his father wished him to go to the USA, when he had just started at a new school. This was in February 1964, during the first week of Sellers' marriage to Britt. Whereupon, his father asked him, '"Who do you love most – me or your mother?" Knowing he would be angered, I spat out, "I love Mummy best".' At this, Sellers 'went berserk', saying, 'You can pack your things now. You're going back to your mother's and I never want to see you again.' Sarah, however, who 'had already got the drift of things,' replied more tactfully, telling her father, 'I love you both the same.'[14] However, not long afterwards, Sellers invited both children to the USA for a holiday and to visit Disneyland.[15]

In 1965, Michael, now aged 11, was sent to boarding school at Frensham Heights, which was not far from the family home at Elstead. However, he said, 'some nights I would secretly slip away and return home on the bus.' When this was discovered, and it was likely that Michael would be expelled from school, his father told him, 'Don't worry about it.' Michael was duly expelled.[16]

Michael was sent to see a psychiatrist, who reported that he was 'an insecure child lacking the attention of his father'. Said he,

> Later, as my conduct at school showed no signs of improving, he diagnosed that I was going through an identity crisis and that my disruptive practices in the classroom were made in order to get

attention. The psychologist was getting closer to the truth. I no longer wanted to be Peter Sellers' son. I craved for my own identity. What had Dad done for me? Did he really care about me? Whenever I talked about school to him, he was always too busy to listen. His own activities and pursuits left him no time to spare for anyone else, not even his children.

Michael now became a pupil at King Alfred's co-educational school, Golders Green, where his sister Sarah would subsequently join him.[17]

Michael accepted an invitation to 'arrange the stage lighting for the school's 50th anniversary pageant', when he had already promised to spend the weekend with his father. Sellers reacted in a characteristic childish and petulant manner. 'Tell me the truth, Michael. You don't love me. You don't want to come to see me. Why invent excuses? If that's how you feel about me then I have no wish to see you again. Is that understood? Stay at school. Stay wherever you like. But don't come home to me.'[18]

Michael explained how, 'to be a friend of Dad was like running an assault course with no finishing line.' Potential friends 'must all have known they were going to be insulted and abused. Anyone who could stand up after that kind of treatment and remain loyal to him was indeed a true friend.'[19]

Sellers told Michael that he wished him to be a film director, but Michael eventually became a carpenter, 'spurning the glamorous lifestyle that he wanted me to follow'. Whereupon, his father asked him when he was 'going to get a "real job"'.[20] As for Sarah, from King Alfred's school, 'she went on to study art: first at Camberwell and then at the City and Guild in Kennington. She always sought Dad's approval, but as I myself had experienced, his interest in what she was doing was vague.'[21]

Said Michael of his father, 'As a youngster I was the apple of his eye – the son and heir of whom he was so proud. My mother has often said to me that she doesn't know what happened and when, but suddenly he turned off.'[22]

For example, Sellers had arranged a trust fund to be set up in favour of Sarah and Michael, but when they both thanked him for this 'on a number of occasions', he denied that they had done so. 'Retribution came swiftly,' said Michael, 'we both got letters from Dad disowning us.' The letters, which were identically worded, read, 'Whatever relationship we might have had is finished, the time has come for you to continue your own way. I no longer wish to be thought of as your father.'[23]

Michael summed up the situation thus: 'My father was a very difficult man to be with. You had to be whatever he wanted you to be at the time. He didn't make any allowances for you; *you* had to make allowances for him. If you didn't, then you were instant history.'[24]

Why *did* Sellers change so dramatically in his attitude to his children? This is a question of great significance, and it will be discussed shortly.

Chapter 12

Sellers' Core Beliefs

In the case of a person such as Sellers, whose life was very largely an act, is it possible to discover what his core beliefs were? Yes, because there are clues along the way.

In the late 1950s, long before he became famous, Sellers, as already mentioned, featured in two gramophone record albums, *The Best of Sellers* (1958) and *Songs for Swingin' Sellers* (1959). On the jacket sleeve of the latter album, it stated humorously that 'For Maximum Enjoyment, only use needles of Burmese plywood'; 'Wind the gramophone and stand it in an empty zinc bath'; 'Point the horn due south and tilt it at an angle of 37 degrees (fahr.) to the perpendicular'; 'Send Grandma out of the room'. Clearly, a treat was in store!

Hypocrisy is the practice of claiming to have higher standards or more laudable beliefs than is the case; flummery means empty compliments or nonsense.[1] Sellers was a master at exposing such human traits, by way of satire, defined as the use of humour, irony, exaggeration, or ridicule to expose and criticise people's stupidity or vices.

> Irony: the expression of meaning through the use of language signifying the opposite, typically for humorous effect. Lampoon – to publicly satirise or ridicule.
>
> Parody: imitation for comic effect.[2]

Vicariously, through the characters that he played and with the use of the above techniques, Sellers took a tremendous swipe at society, and what he considered to be some of its more disingenuous aspects. For example, hypocrisy ('Lord Badminton' in his 'Memoirs'); pretentiousness ('Nancy Spain' in 'The Critics'); exploitation ('Major Ralph Ralph' in 'The Contemporary Scene 1'); the politician (in 'Party Political Speech').

Towards the end of his career, he would take another massive swipe at many of the values of so-called 'western civilisation', in a film called *Being There*, as will be seen.

Examples taken from the two aforementioned albums are as follows.

From *The Best of Sellers* (1958)

'Balham! Gateway to the South!'
(Written by Frank Muir and Dennis Norden.
Performed by Sellers.)

Frank H. Muir (1920–1998) was an English comedy writer and radio and television personality. Denis M. Norden (1922–2018) was an English comedy writer and TV presenter. Muir and Norden had an association lasting for more than fifty years.

Here, Sellers delights in ridiculing the alleged attractions of the fictitious English town, 'Balham', and the pretentiousness of those who promote it. In fact, on closer inspection, everything is underwhelming and a let-down.

> We enter Balham through the verdant grasslands of Battersea Park, and at once we are aware that here is a land of happy, contented people who go about their daily tasks in truly democratic spirit.
>
> This is a busy High Street, focal point of the town's activities. Note the quaint old stores, whose frontage is covered with hand-painted inscriptions, every one a rare example of native Balham art. Let us read some of them as our camera travels past:
>
> Cooking apples! Choice eaters!
> A song to remember at the Tantamount Cinema!
> A suit to remember at Montague Moss
> Cremations conducted with decorum and taste.
> Frying tonight. Bring your own paper.
>
> This shows the manifold activities of Balham's thriving community – but in quiet corners, we still find examples of the exquisite workmanship that Balham craftsmen have made world-famous: toothbrush holesmanship:

'On my forge, I carve the little holes in the top of toothbrushes. It is exciting work and my forefathers have been engaged upon it since 1957.'

So much for Balham's industries. Now let us see a little more of the town. Here is the great park, covering nearly half an acre. This is where the children traditionally meet by the limpid waters of the old drinking fountain, a drinking fountain that has for countless years, across the vast aeons of time, give untold pleasure to man, woman and child. The fountain was 'donated by Councillor Quills as long ago as 1928'.

We are now entering Old Balham. Time has passed by this remote corner; so shall we. But Balham is not neglecting the cultural side. This is Eugene Quills, whose weekly recitals are attended by a vast concourse of people. He has never had a lesson in his life. Such is the enthusiasm of Balham's music lovers that they are subscribing to a fund to send Eugene to Italy. Or Vienna. Or anywhere!

Night falls on Balham: From Quills' Folly, Balham's famous beauty spot, which stands nearly 10 feet above sea level, the town is spread below us in a fairyland of glittering lights, changing all the time: green... amber... red... red and amber... and back to green. The night life is awakening!

At the 'Al Morocco' Tea Rooms, a conversation is overheard:

'Hey, miss?'
'Yes? What d'you want?'
'Pilchards.'
'They're off, dear'
'Oh! Baked beans?'
'Off.'
'Oh! Meat? – meat loaf salad?'
'That's off, too.'
'Pot of tea?'
'No tea, dear.'
'Well, just milk then.'
'Milk's off.'
'Roll and butter, then?'

'No butter, dear.'
'Well, just a roll!'
'Only bread, love.'
'I might have just as well have stayed at home!'
'Oh, I dunno, does you good to have a fling occasionally!'

And so, the long night draws on. The last stragglers make their way home and the lights go out one by one as dawn approaches and the bell of Saint Quills' Parish Church tolls ten o'clock. Balham sleeps. And so, we say farewell to this historic borough, with many pleasant memories – and the words of C. Quills Smith, Balham's own bard, burning in our ears:

> Broad-bosomed, bold, becalmed, benign
> Lies Balham, four-square on the Northern Line.
> Matched by no marvel save in Eastern scene
> A rose-red city, half as gold as green.
> By country churchyard, ferny fen and mere
> What Quills mute inglorious lies buried here?
> Oh, stands the church clock at ten to three
> And is there honey still for tea?
> 'Honey's off, dear.'

This track is notable for its brilliant literary allusions. For example, 'Rose-red city' is taken from the eponymous poem by John William Burgon, in which he describes the Jordanian city of Petra, as a 'Rose red city half as old as time'. 'Is there honey still for tea' is taken from the poem 'The Old Vicarage, Grantchester', by Rupert Brooke: 'Stands the church clock at ten to three? And is there honey still for tea?' The track is also notable for its clever play on words: 'gold as green' i.e. Golders Green!

'Party Political Speech'
(Written by US composer (Martin) Max Schreiner.
Performed by Sellers.)

Here, Sellers lampoons the typical politician, who is fond of the sound of his own voice, but whose utterances are, in fact, utterly vacuous!

Vacuous: showing lack of thought or intelligence.[3]

The politician addresses his audience as follows, in a droning, monotonous voice:

> 'My friends, in the light of present-day developments let me say right away that I do not regard existing conditions likely. On the contrary, I have always regarded them as subjects of the gravest responsibility and shall ever continue to do so. Indeed, I will even go further and state quite categorically that I am more than sensible of the definition of the precise issues which are at this very moment concerning us all. We must build, but we must build surely.'
> 'Hear, hear!'
> 'Let me say just this: If any part of what I am saying is challenged, then I am more than ready to meet such a challenge. For I have no doubt whatsoever, that whatever I may have said in the past, or what I am saying now, is the exact, literal and absolute truth as to the state of the case.'
> 'Hear, hear!'
> 'I put it to you that this is not the time for vague promises of better things to come. For, if I were to convey to you a spirit of false optimism, then I should be neither fair to you nor true to myself. But does this mean, I hear you cry, that we can no longer look forward to the future that is to come? Certainly not!'

When someone in the audience shouts out, 'What about the workers?' and the politician attempts to reply, a fight breaks out! Nevertheless, the politician is undeterred:

'What about the workers indeed sir! Grasp, I beseech you, with both hands, the opportunities that are offered. Let us assume a bold front and go forward together. Let us carry the fight against ignorance to the four corners of the earth, because it is a fight which concerns us all. Now, finally my friends, in conclusion, let me say just this...'

In fact, he had said not a word of any significance!

From *Songs for Swingin' Sellers* (1959)

'The Contemporary Scene – 1: Lord Badminton's Memoirs'
(Written by Schreiner and English composer and conductor Ron A. Goodwin. Performed by Sellers.)

'Nowadays,' says Lord Badminton (a.k.a. Sellers),

it is the custom to think of the aristocracy and leisured classes of Edwardian days as being devoted to little elfs, besides selfish pleasures and amusements. This simply was not the case, and I would like in the next few minutes to attempt to destroy this fallacy.

As a very young boy some of my earliest recollections are of being taken by my father, in those days Chancellor of the Exchequer, on the occasional tours of the estate at Charters. In the course of these expeditions it was his practice to visit those among his poorer tenants and employees who by reasons of accident, old age or sheer carelessness happened to be destitute and nearly starving. Dear, faithful Elliott the coachman, would invariably accompany us carrying an enormous wicker basket which was covered with a dazzling white cloth and containing bowls of dripping and cold stock, cabbage stalks, potato peelings and other nutritious kitchen scraps. As well as these material comforts my father also distributed cracks [jokes] of an improving and uplifting nature which he wrote himself and had printed at his own expense.

Father and son now embark on a visit to the sick bed of 'an ancient and decrepit wagoner' who has 'somehow managed to get himself badly trampled underfoot while attempting to stop a runaway horse and cart.' In an effort to acknowledge his master, the old man raises himself up on his pillow, but,

> with a sickeningly thud which I can hear to this very day, the grizzled pate came into smart contact with an oak beam which curved down just above the bed. With a low moan the unhappy man fell back stunned onto his pillow. He never regained consciousness. Distressed as we were at this incident, my father and I offered a word of cheer to the wagoner's wife and we pressed upon her a basket full of rotten apples and a bundle of cracks before proceeding on our philanthropic way. 'A most merciful release,' observed my father, after the wagoner's funeral. 'Why, he might have lingered on in a bedridden condition for many years, a misery to himself and a burden to others. Providence works in many strange ways.'

Throughout the narrative, the son remembers his father variously as 'First Lord of the Admiralty'; 'President of the Board of Trade'; 'Chancellor of the Exchequer'. He states that Lord Badminton would have attended the wagoner's funeral, 'but for a sudden attack of gout which kept him in bed on the day.' The son concludes, 'I hope that in relating this anecdote, that I have indicated something of the wonderful sort of relationship that existed between the family at the Hall and the peasantry on the estate.'

'The Contemporary Scene – 1: The Critics'
(Written by Schreiner and Goodwin.
Performed by Sellers and British character actress Irene Handl.)

Here, Sellers and Irene poke fun at the critics, as they review material that is almost completely obscure and in a jargon which hardly anybody understands!

In the role of chairman, Sellers introduces the programme.

> Good afternoon. Today we have with us in the studio Newton Tweedsdale, art critic of *The Onlooker*; J. Wallace Larwood, book critic of *The New Politician*, and Faith Bradshaw, film critic of the *Sunday Sun*.

This week we have all been to see the exhibition of paintings by August Stepnopolikas Bonstart at the Royal Tate.

What did the panel think of the exhibition? Tweedsdale [Sellers], in his affected way, opines that

> Bonstart is always exciting, isn't he, isn't he? And I am bound to say that I enjoyed the exhibition immensely. Nonetheless [he smacks his lips], one thing did strike me rather forcibly. To me at any rate, to me at any rate, his later work did seem to suffer from a lack of cosmic awareness which is entirely opposite with the more obvious sensibilities of his more useful canvasses. One can now detect in Bonstart's work a certain architectural [further smacking of lips], yes architectural, architectural as well as lyrical quality of suspensive secrecy with regard to paint and brushwork; a sense of fossilised motion which seems almost literally to spring, spring, spring at one, from some of the paintings.

Faith Bradshaw [Irene Handl] opines that

> sensing the resurgence of the traditional stress was exactly what Bonstart has done and is doing. I should have also said that he habitually used angular fragmentation of pigment in order to consummate his all-pervading theme of hermetic anarchy. It's as simple as that!

Says Wallis Larwood [Sellers],

> I know so little about art any way, I'm afraid I'm rather out of my depth here. I can only say that I was strangely impressed by what I saw. It thus may appear fanciful but at times the nature of the work seems so embarrassingly personal that one almost gets the feeling that one was intruding.

The chairman concludes that

> Yes, we appear to be agreed on essentials here and divided only on minor points. Now the book which we have all been reading is the

new novel, *The Seeds of Distress* by Luigi Salami, published by Bodley Hamilton at 15 shillings.

But it unfortunately transpires that two of the critics have been reading different books, and as for Larwood, 'I'm afraid nobody told me to read anything at all!' he says.

'My Old Dutch'
(Lyrics by English music hall comedian Albert Chevalier. Music composed by his brother Auguste Chevalier under the pseudonym Charles Ingle. Performed by Sellers.)

Here, Sellers highlights the hypocritical and over-sentimental nature of those who purport to be devoted to their spouses, as opposed to the reality of the situation.

This song is sung by Sellers in a romanticised manner that becomes even more emotionally charged as the song progresses, until he almost breaks down in tears:

> I've got a pal, a regular out an' outer.
> She's a dear good old gal,
> An' I'll tell you all about 'er;
> It's many years since first we met,
> Her hair was then as black as jet.
> It's whiter now, but she don't fret
> Not my old gal
> We've been together now for forty years
> And it don't seem a day too much.
> 'Cause there ain't a lady living in the land
> As I'd swap for my dear old Dutch.
> No, there ain't a lady living in the land
> As I'd swap for my dear old Dutch.

However, when the 'Old Dutch' suddenly appears and starts gabbling in the Dutch language, 'Get back in the kitchen you rotten old Dutch person,' he cries.

Here, Sellers is poking fun of the fact that men tend to put their spouses on a pedestal, but when they appear in the flesh, the way they treat them is rather different! The same could probably be said of women in relation to men.

'So Little Time'
(Written by Muir and Norden. Performed by Sellers.)

Here, the interviewee is 'Miss Nancy Lisbon' – clearly a take-off of real-life broadcaster and journalist Nancy Brooker Spain. She interviews 'Major Ralph [first name pronounced 'Raif'] Ralph', both parts being played by Sellers.

Major Ralph is described as, 'the colourful horse dealer who'd gone into the business of managing rock and roll stars'. He personally discovered such disc names as 'Lenny Bronze', 'Clint Thigh' and 'Matt Lust' and such vocal groups as 'The Fleshpots' and 'The Muckrakers'. 'These rock and roll boys are big business now,' he says.

'But it must be so very different, going from horse trading to rock and roll singers?' says Miss Lisbon.

'Well it is. Horses have got a better ear for music,' replies the major. 'Have you ever seen a rock and roll singer Miss Lisbon? I mean have you ever seen one up close?'

'I'm mostly on book reviewing.'

'Good specimen, about 17 or 18 years old, about 5 foot 10 fully extended, sagging to about 5 foot 4 in the sitting position. Points to look for are the forehead, shouldn't be more than half an inch of that, plenty of mouth, the lower lip permanently slack and beware of possible fallen arches. This saves a lot of trouble in mid career you know.'

'I suppose a nice musical singing voice is what you look out for as well is it?'

'Huh! By jove yes! First sight of that and out he goes, what?'

Miss Lisbon is surprised to learn that five or six of these rock and roll stars live with Major Ralph in his own home.

'It's not all that eccentric,' says the major. 'I mean some of them can be house trained with a bit of patience. Would you like to see one, I'll get one for you.'

The rock star appears, saying, 'Major, some rotten 'o's' pinched the strings of my guitar, look!'

'It's on back to front. How many more times must I tell you the hole points away from you!'

When asked his name, he replies, 'Cyril Rumbold,' whereupon the major responds irritably, 'Not your real name, the name I gave you!'

'Ah, Twit Conway.'

This is a take-off of a US country music singer, stage name 'Conway Twitty'. Twit says that he can't walk very fast, because his 'crepe soles are so high off the ground!' Furthermore, his jeans are so tight that his kneecaps have gone 'all green', obliging him to release the pressure by making holes in the material. Whereupon, Major Ralph lends him his fountain pen to 'ink in where the flesh shows!'

'Hello! I'm a journalist,' says Miss Lisbon, and 'I should so much like to do a story on you as a person. Tell me, what does it feel like to suddenly find yourself a teenage idol?'

'Well, ah, it don't make much difference really. I mean, I was idle before I was a teenager.'

'No! No!' interjects the major. 'What the lad is trying to say is that success has not spoiled him. He's still the same twit he always was, right lad?' He tells Twit to remember what he's been taught to say when answering press questions. 'Tell Miss Lisbon how you look after your parents, Conway.'

'Who?'

'Your parents! Your mother and father!'

'Oh yeah. Now that I've got money, I've been able to move my old mum and dad into a small house.'

'I bet they're delighted!' says Miss Lisbon.

'No, they ain't! They was in a big house. It was the Major's idea you see, he said you evict them, and I'll flog the...' At that point there's sound of a blow being struck.

'Well, Conway, back you go to your quarters,' instructs the major. 'Tell Vincent Donney I'll be along in a moment for some hip twitching practice.'

Before she goes, the major entreats Miss Lisbon not to write one of those

The author and his friend Robert Norcliffe, who watched their first Peter Sellers 'Pink Panther' film together whilst undergraduates at Oxford in 1964

96, Castle Road, Southsea, Hampshire, birthplace of Peter Sellers. He would have been amused to see that, when this photograph was taken, the building was home to a Chinese restaurant! (*Wikimedia Commons*)

Cottages on Muswell Hill Road, London. The one with the blue plaque was the childhood home of Peter Sellers. (*Chris Whippet, Wikimedia Commons*)

Peg and Bill Sellers. (*Associated Newspapers*)

The Grafton Arms, 2 Strutton Ground, London. (*Wikimedia Commons*)

The Goon Show, Volume 29, 'We're in the Wrong House Again' (Audio CD, BBC Physical Audio, 5 April 2012)

The Best of Sellers, Parlophone, Vinyl, 1958

Songs for Swingin' Sellers, Parlophone, Vinyl, 1959

Peter Sellers, circa 1975. (*Wikimedia Commons*)

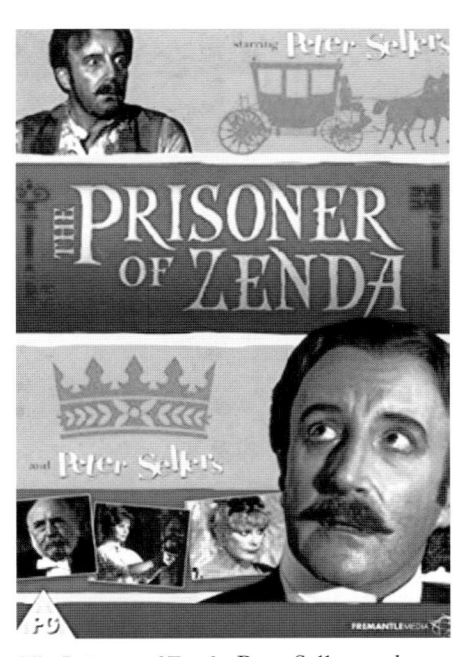

The Prisoner of Zenda, Peter Sellers and Lynne Frederick (DVD, 2008)

Being There (DVD jacket cover, Warner Brothers, 2002)

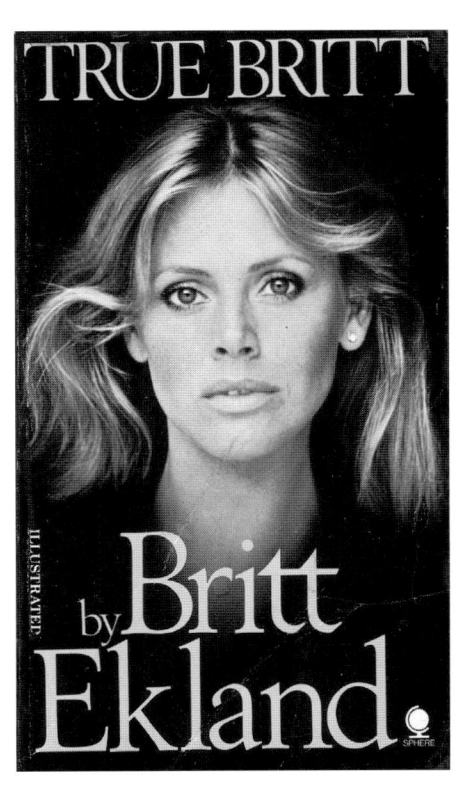

True Britt, by Britt Ekland, jacket cover (London, Sphere, 1980)

Being There, Peter Sellers and Shirley MacLaine (DVD jacket cover, Warner Brothers, 2002)

William Parnell (Guild of British Film Editors), working on the film *Greystoke: The Legend of Tarzan, Lord of the Apes* in 1983. (Robert Hambling)

P.S. I Love You, by Michael Sellers, jacket cover (London, Collins, 1991)

P.S. I Love You, by Michael Sellers: jacket cover rear, featuring Sellers' son Michael and his daughters Sarah and Victoria

Spotted in the author's favourite caf in Poole, Dorset, UK a visitor, showing the enduring popularity of 'The Pink Panther (Ivor McNeill)

nasty lurid stories about my kids. You saw Conway for yourself, just as normal and well balanced as any other 17-year-old ex-plasterer's mate suddenly earning a 1,000 quid a week. And don't you go making me out to be a sort of profiteering Svengali. These boys stay here willingly, because to them I'm a sort of almost a second father. We have a beautiful relationship, beautiful Miss Lisbon because it is based on trust, mutual trust.

'A very rare quality in this modern world, Major.'

'It is indeed, yes. Oh, don't touch the doorknob, it's got 2,000 volts running through it.'

'The Contemporary Scene 2'
(Written by Schreiner and Goodwin. Performed by Sellers.)

Here, Sellers plays the part of the type of interviewer with whom everyone is familiar, one who is utterly disinterested in what the interviewee has to say, and is determined at all costs to prevent him or her from saying it!

The interviewee is the unfortunate Mr Harris, who is bombarded by questions:

I have a feeling that you're trying to sidestep the issue. There is a rumour now gaining ground in certain circles that for a man in the centre of public affairs your life is perhaps not all that it should be. Now is there any substantial truth in this? I'm going to be quite blunt with you and in return I expect you to be equally so. Now tell me, am I right in thinking that you are in fact a homo … And is it not also true that you are a lifelong member of the Communist Party? I am only seeking a simple and straightforward answer to what I think you must admit is a simple and straightforward question. Can we be serious, for one moment!

By this time Mr Harris is reduced to a nervous and frustrated wreck and complains that, 'I haven't said anything yet!' To which the reply comes, 'I suggest that you are deliberately trying to withhold information rather than reveal it. Thank you, Mr Harris!'

Ironically, Sellers himself, when he came to fame, would find himself subjected to similar indignities, when he was interviewed in a similar way by the insufferable 'Brylcreem and bluster' brigade of interviewers, who show off, do not listen, do not follow the conversation, and as a result, fire off one non-sequitur after another. As that exemplary interviewer Michael Parkinson once observed dryly, 'In my day, the interview was about the interviewee.'

Conclusion

The above tracks, and others contained in the two albums *The Best of Sellers* and *Songs for Swingin' Sellers* gave Sellers the opportunity to mock those whom he considered to be insincere. The tracks clearly appealed to him greatly, and this gives an early and unique insight into the way his own mind was working at that time. For surely he would not have accepted such roles had he not empathised with the message that they were attempting to portray. In other words, at that time of his life he saw pretentiousness, snobbery, hypocrisy, showing off, etc. for precisely what it was.

In my own lifetime, I have encountered numerous similar instances of falseness, usually associated with politicians, and certain phrases, which have become notorious, spring to mind:

> 'It is time to return to those core values, time to get back to basics, to self-discipline.'

This was said by British prime minister John Major in 1993; who, between 1984 and 1988, had conducted an affair with Conservative MP and minister Edwina Currie, who like him was also married.

> 'If it falls to me to start a fight to cut out the cancer of bent and twisted journalism in our country, with the simple sword of truth and the trusty shield of fair play, so be it! I am ready for the fight!'

This was said by Conservative MP Jonathan Aitken on the 10 April 1995. Four years later, Aitken was convicted of perjury and received an eighteen-month prison sentence.

Some years ago, a friend of mine attended a concert in Hyde Park where a famous folk singer sang songs bewailing the fate of the poor and underprivileged. At the end, there was a three-hour queue simply to get out of the car park. The singer left in his private helicopter!

Today, we have people affecting concern about global warming, while at the same time they travel thousands of miles by air to attend climate change conferences. We have Conservative politicians stating that theirs is the party of law and order when knife crime on the streets of the UK is completely out of control. We have a former prime minister advertising the fact that he is following a 'green agenda' as he goes to work on his bicycle. Meanwhile, a motor vehicle is travelling behind him carrying his briefcase! When Labour politicians use the term 'working people', what they really mean are members of trade unions.

In later life, and perhaps bearing in mind what little good the acquisition of wealth had done for him in terms of lasting personal happiness, Sellers would direct his fire and withering sarcasm against another target and mount a devastating attack on the West's obsession with money and materialism.

Chapter 13

Generosity and Acts of Kindness

Having met Sellers in late 1949, said Milligan, 'I became a very close friend of his. He took a great liking to me. I was pretty homeless at the time: my mother and father had gone to Australia and I didn't have a home, so I slept on the floor in his bedroom on a pumped-up mattress. He stayed [i.e., he was living] with his mother, who doted on him.'[1] Furthermore, Sellers, he said, was 'instrumental in getting me into the BBC,' i.e. as script writer and performer in *The Goon Show*. 'He was very kind like that.'

'He really was generous,' said Geldray. 'If there was something I wanted, all I had to do was say a word and he would buy it. Eventually, I gave up mentioning a lot of things to avoid this happening.'[2] When Geldray had an operation on his leg, Sellers got to hear about it. Whereupon, he visited him at home and insisted that Geldray got into his new car that was parked outside. 'But I can't walk,' said Geldray. 'I'll carry you!' replied Sellers.

> And he did. He lifted me from the living room all the way into his car. We went round to a shopping centre. He told me to wait in the car and listen to the radio, and this I did – for a long time. Eventually, he returned, followed by a man laden with parcels. Peter told me, 'They're for you'. When we got home, we undid them and they made up a complete new sound system, turntable and every extra you can think of.[3]

Continued Geldray, Sellers 'used to call me when he wanted to go downtown in London. He would say "I'm going to the camera shop" – which he did all the time – "and why don't you come with me?" One particular time he said, "I'll pick you up in ten minutes".'

When the two of them visited the shop, Sellers admired 'a new and very small Swiss camera'. But when he offered to buy it for Geldray, he declined. Whereupon, he said, 'several hours later, I opened the door of my home, and in the middle of the living room was a package. I opened it, and there was the new Swiss camera.'[4]

During the mid-1960s, said Lodge, when Sellers was married to Britt, Sellers discovered that

> my mother was stricken with cancer. He was due to go out with Princess Margaret and Tony [Anthony Armstrong Jones] that night but he held everything and told me to leave it to him. He arranged it all. The next day, she was in Harley Street with top people, and Peter picked up the tab. But it wasn't really a question of money. Peter wanted to help my mother. He gave her another fifteen months of life.[5]

Actress Françoise Pascal worked with Sellers in the 1970 film *There's a Girl in My Soup*, where he starred as Robert Danvers and she played the part of Paola. On the afternoon of 21 February 1970, when Françoise was at the home of actress Viviane Ventura, a fire broke out and Françoise was obliged to jump from the third-floor window. Said she, 'I was taken, unconscious, to St George's Hospital in Belgravia. On my second day in hospital, I vaguely remembered this Indian doctor coming to see me, sitting by my bed and talking to me.' This was Sellers in disguise, 'dressed as an Indian doctor so as not to be recognised by the press'.

When Françoise became fully conscious, she found a rose and a card on her bedside from Sellers. 'The thoughtfulness of this man was tremendous, and he gave me a will to get up and get better.' Sellers subsequently

> telephoned several times to enquire about my health. I will never forget his kindness towards me in those hard times.[6] Peter was a marvellous man. I sat many evenings with him in his flat in Belgravia, listening to his Indian music and listening to him talking in an Indian voice, and generally having a good laugh. I used to see him very relaxed, and he was great to be with. I love him to bits as a friend and miss his sense of humour and his kindness.[7]

The film *Hoffman* (1970) was directed by Canadian Alvin Rakoff, who said that on the last day of shooting Sellers

> arrived with gifts for everybody. He gave the camera operator a color television set – that was pretty rare in 1969. He gave Leica cameras, tape recorders, small portable radios. His factotum, Bert [Mortimer], distributed them. As for Rakoff himself, and the film's British producer Ben Arbeid, he invited them to take a holiday of their choice anywhere in the world, together with their wives, 'and send me the bill'.[8]

According to Bert Mortimer, said Sikov, Sellers 'liked to prowl London parks at night looking for homeless people. When he found an appropriate one, he'd stuff a £5 note in his pocket. Bert witnessed these transactions: "You'd see the man flinch back, thinking he was going to be hit, then fish out the note and stare in utter disbelief at it".'[9]

Finally, said Michael of his father, 'Dad didn't ever forget his chums, whenever he made a film. If there was a part he knew would suit a friend, he would suggest their name for it.'[10]

Chapter 14

Nostalgia

Said Anne Levy, whenever anything awful happened to her husband Sellers, he became very nostalgic.

> He used to love doing these tours of all the things that happened to him during his life, and he would say 'That's where I went to school and met my first love'. He was then 7 years of age. And then he would take me to his school, St Aloysius, Highgate: 'Saint Alley Wash Out' as he called it. And he would tell me all about that, sitting outside the school.[1]

When Sellers' mother Peg died in 1967, Anne had by then been 'happily' remarried to Ted Levy for four years. 'I had a little shop, and he [Sellers] came round there and he said, "Please, I just want you to come out in the car," and I just had to go and do a tour of all the old places.'[2]

Said Michael,

> My father never fully let go of people and things from the past, as if sensing they represented a more sane time before the madness of success was thrust upon him. He had this curious nature whereby he would discard everything as he continued his journey through life, but then like[d] to go back just to have a sneaky look. Not just friends, but old houses and theatres. He wanted to float among the ghosts of yesteryear.[3]

In late 1972, said Michael, Sellers embarked on 'nostalgic pilgrimages' to his parents' former home in Portsmouth, once more to his old school in Highgate and to the Grafton Arms, 'where the Goons were first formed'. On one such journey, Sellers was accompanied by 'a schoolday sweetheart – the girl who bore his illegitimate child'. Sellers had previously told his children that he 'had an illegitimate daughter whom he had not seen since her adoption'. Michael gave no further details.[4]

In the summer of 1974 the new owner of Brookfield, a Mr Stead, noticed Sellers standing by the front gate. 'I'm just looking at the garden,' he said. Whereupon, Stead invited him to walk around the garden, which he did 'for half an hour or so.' As he was leaving, Sellers studied the walnut tree and told the owner that the holes in its bark had been made by his son Michael, with lead pellets from his air gun. 'I wonder if I could bring Michael back here one day, I would really like him to see the house now,' said Sellers.[5]

Michael referred to Sellers being affected by 'the madness of success'. But was there another reason, other than achieving success, to explain why Sellers had been happy in his youth, yet unhappy in adulthood? This will be discussed shortly.

Chapter 15

Some Notable Film and Stage Appearances

In the film *The Ladykillers* (1955), Alec Guinness was cast as Professor Marcus and Sellers as Harry, a.k.a. Mr Robinson, a small-time crook. Guinness, said film critic Derek Malcolm, was someone who Sellers 'adored and whom he got on very well with. And I think he took a lot of advice from Alec Guinness who was very helpful to him during the film.'[1] Michael agreed, saying that Guinness, 'was to exercise considerable influence over Dad, who practically became his protégé.'[2]

Secombe described how the only time that he, Milligan, and Sellers appeared on stage together was in November 1955 at the Hippodrome Theatre in Coventry. At that time, Sellers 'was experimenting with all kinds of comic ideas because he hated doing the same act night after night.'[3]

In 1958, Peter Hall invited Sellers to appear as the Sultan in the West End stage play *Brouhaha*, a comedy by Hungarian dramatist George Tabori, which opened on 27 August. Hall described how, in the theatre, one has to repeat the same performance to the best of one's ability night after night. He said, 'Peter couldn't bear doing it again and again and again.'[4] Said Dennis Selinger, 'He really doesn't like theatre; he doesn't like the discipline of it.' Hall and Selinger might also have used the word 'boredom', because someone with Sellers' vivid imagination would have found the repetitive churning out of the same play utterly stultifying after the first performance. Also, said Bentine, Sellers 'dreaded having to play straight,' i.e. serious drama.[5]

Curiously, despite the fact that being a theatre actor was anathema to Sellers, said Secombe, 'He had no stage fright. He was not a man like the rest of us who'd stand in the wings trembling. He was completely calm, and that was a feature of him which I found quite disturbing in a way.'[6] This seemingly innocuous observation by Secombe is highly significant and it reveals perhaps more about Sellers than any other, for this reason.

When acting and thus adopting the persona of a character different from his own, all his anxiety, self-doubt, and feelings of worthlessness melted instantaneously away. Now, he felt and safe and secure. But had he been required to appear in public as himself, he would have been petrified. This will be discussed in more detail shortly.

In the 1959 black and white comedy, *The Battle of the Sexes*, Sellers featured as Mr Martin, the head accountant for a Scottish weaving company. His assistant was Mr Meekie, played by Abe Barker. As Meekie writes in the ledger with his squeaky pen, Mr Martin looks up with a pained expression and asks, 'Mr Meekie, would you try to find a quieter nib please?' Sellers' sense of the hilariously absurd and his perfect timing were present even in those early days!

The Boulting brothers, John and Ray, made a string of films: satirical comedies ridiculing the British class system. For example, *I'm All Right Jack* (1959), where Sellers plays the pompous shop steward Fred Kite. When Sellers read the script, he asked, 'Where are the jokes? Where are the laughs?' Said Ray Boulting, 'we had to explain, we were not asking him to play the part of a "Goon".'[7] In 1960, for his portrayal of Kite, Sellers won a BAFTA (British Academy of Film and Television Arts) best British actor award.

In the film *Two Way Stretch* (1960) in which he plays Dodger Lane, a young criminal who is serving a prison sentence, Sellers may have imagined that he was back at home, being waited on by his mother Peg, as his fellow inmates bring the newspaper to him in his prison cell, make his breakfast, and shut the window because, in his words, there was 'a bit of a George Raft' (Cockney slang for draught) coming in. 'I see the bottom's dropped out of colonial cocoa,' he says.

In *Only Two Can Play* (1962), Sellers' own past marital difficulties were echoed when he played the part of librarian John Lewis, who had fallen under the spell of Liz (Mai Zetterling), wife of a local councillor, much to the dismay and consternation of his wife Jean.

Dr Strangelove, or How I Learned to Stop Worrying and Love the Bomb (1964) was filmed at Shepperton Studios, Surrey. The film was a devastating satire on the nuclear arms race. Sellers played not only Dr Strangelove himself, but also the President of the USA, and an English RAF group captain. The film was produced by Stanley Kubrick (who had also directed *Lolita*).

In *What's New Pussy Cat?* (1965) Sellers played the role of a psychiatrist, which was perhaps ironic, in the sense that in many people's opinion, it was *he* who probably needed psychiatric treatment![8]

Sellers invited Scottish film director Joe McGrath to direct *Casino Royale* (1967) but insisted that fellow actor Orson Welles never appeared in the same frame as himself. Presumably, he was afraid that Welles would steal the limelight. 'Well, that's stupid!' said McGrath. 'Apart from anything else, the whole value of the film is having you and Orson together, and also it's being filmed in Panavision [a film company producing widescreen films]!' Sellers accused McGrath of deserting him. 'He swung a punch at me,' said McGrath, 'and I thought, well I'd better swing a punch back or I shall never live this down, so I swung a punch at him as well. We made up and were friends again.' Whereupon, Sellers said, "I'm going off to make a phone call," and he disappeared for three weeks!'[9]

In *Soft Beds: Hard Battles* (1974), Sellers played six parts. This was two less than the eight parts played by Alec Guinness in the film *Kind Hearts and Coronets* (1949).

In *The Prisoner of Zenda* (1979), Sellers played three roles, including that of Prince Rudolph, whose bride, Princess Flavia, was played by his then wife, Lynne.

Sellers' final project was the film *The Fiendish Plot of Dr Fu Manchu* (1980), featuring the eponymous 168-year-old doctor, played by Sellers, who was searching for the elixir that would give eternal life. (In the film, Sellers also played Nayland Smith, an English country gentleman detective.)

Chapter 16

Insecurity and the Need to Escape

Said Derek Malcolm of Sellers,

> He was an insecure, lonely boy dominated by his mother. He was someone who thought of himself as a solitary person, who somehow had to be other people in order to get noticed. He felt he was nobody. He wanted to become somebody, and the only way he could do it was through being somebody else on the screen, and he did that absolutely brilliantly.[1]

Anne Levy concurred with this view. 'He couldn't relax; he couldn't go on holiday, couldn't really just be himself. He was only happy when he was playing a part.'[2]

David Lodge, who worked on many films with Sellers, stated that he first met him in early 1945 whilst he was serving in the RAF and performing in the *Gang Show*. Lodge spoke of Sellers' 'desire to be someone else. His insecurity stemmed from the fact that he wasn't happy with who he was: he was only happy when he pulled on another character.'[3]

Sellers himself admitted as much. For example, Sikov quoted him as saying, 'As soon as I can get into some character I'm away. I use the characters to protect myself, as a shield – like getting into a hut and saying, "nobody can see me".'[4]

His father also attempted to distance himself physically from difficult situations, said Michael. When things got 'sticky', his response 'was to move on, he moved off somewhere else. The neighbours are crap so let's move on, let's sell the car, move on, you escape.'[5]

Escapism is defined as the tendency to seek distraction and relief from unpleasant realities, especially by seeking entertainment or engaging in fantasy.[6] Sellers' insecurity meant that he was always seeking ways to escape into a safer world, either through the characters that he played or in other ways, such as having a change of scene, or even a change of wife!

Actor David Lodge, described how, when they were in the RAF together, Sellers once dressed up as a lieutenant, even though he held 'the very lowest rank in the RAF, viz "Aircraftman", and said he was going to the Officers Mess. A fellow *Gang Show* member [had] obtained the uniform from the *Gang Show*'s make-up box, complete with medal ribbons and the staff [swagger stick].' Whereupon, Sellers donned the uniform and announced that he intended to 'inspect the lads downstairs. I think he did it because he didn't like himself as he was. He didn't think he was attractive at all, and he didn't like being a nobody. He wanted to be somebody which he couldn't be, so he pulled on that disguise which later in his professional life became the key to his great success. Because that's what he can do, transform himself into anything he wanted.'[7]

Sellers could mimic any voice, said Secombe, but 'if you asked him to do a "Peter Sellers" voice he couldn't do it. He always had to hide behind something'.[8]

What was at the root of this insecurity? Jonathan Miller, theatre and opera director and actor, spoke about the 'chameleon character' of Sellers: one aspect of which was his 'terror' at being seen merely as

> a nonentity. The chameleon which so enabled him as a performer had a double function: it was a talent which was marketable and something which pleased and delighted an audience; but it was also some sort of sanctuary into which he was able to retreat in order to fight off some sort of demons about which we know nothing, or the hideous knowledge that he might have been, personally, a nonentity.[9]

Said Hattie Proudfoot, 'Every time he moved [house],' and 'whether he was losing a wife or gaining another one, he always came home to roost at the Dorchester,' where he invariably occupied the most expensive 'Oliver Messel' suite.[10] The hotel was clearly a bolt-hole for him.

But for Sellers, such antidotes to insecurity provided at best only temporary relief, and the quest was always on for the happiness and peace of mind that eluded him.

Chapter 17

Low Self-Esteem and its Possible Origins

Those who are familiar with Sellers' films might find it difficult to believe that he possessed low self-esteem. All the more so because, besides his renowned acting ability, in the real world he was gifted with many other talents. For example, he was an accomplished amateur photographer, as Bill Parnell confirmed. Said Milligan with typical humour, 'I had an 8-mm camera, and Peter had a 16-mm camera. He was richer than me, he was richer by 8 millimetres.'[1]

Sellers was an accomplished drummer, ukulele player, and singer. He also enjoyed model-making. Said Anne Levy, 'he used to like making models, he did that with Graham Stark.'[2] Said Stark, 'I think we had the entire American battlefleet built. This was apart from the USS *Saratoga*, which Sellers suddenly realised was missing from his collection, and which he hastily rushed out and purchased the kit for.' Said Anne, 'He said it was for Michael but actually I think it was for himself!'[3]

Sellers possessed enormous charm, but above all, it was his sense of humour and brilliant portrayal of his characters which marked him out. He brought joy and laughter to millions throughout the world, but his low self-esteem meant that he himself always struggled to find happiness and contentment.

Said Anne, 'Peter was two people. There was Peter the actor, and Peter the person. The actor was self-assured and brilliant, and I admired and respected him tremendously. The person, on the other hand, had incredibly low self-esteem and never knew how he should behave. In the end, I could not cope with him.'[4]

Childhood

Sellers, as a child, had many reasons to feel insecure. The family changed its place of residence on many occasions during his childhood, and this would have made it difficult for him to make lasting friendships with his peers, both at school and in his locality, as most children do. Furthermore, having been led to believe that his father was a great achiever (the source of Bill's alleged exploits was probably Bill himself!), this may have given him a sense of inferiority. But what of Bill's relationship with his son?

Interviewed by Michael Parkinson in 1974, Sellers declared, 'Dad was convinced always I was going to be a road sweeper, you see, and he always used to tell me, very encouraging of Dad, "So you'll turn out to be a bloody road sweeper will you? I'll tell you that!"'[5] In other words, in true Yorkshire fashion, Bill Sellers was posing the question before promptly providing the answer himself. In this context, the crucial word is 'always': i.e. this was said by Bill to his son not once, but often. Sellers made light of this during the interview, but it may have significantly affected him later in life.

Sellers was, in effect, sandwiched between a mother who mollycoddled him and did her best to make him totally dependent upon her, whilst at the same time demanding precious little in the way of effort from him in the process; and on the other hand a father who was constantly telling the young man that, when he grew up, he would be fit only to sweep the roads. Yorkshiremen are renowned for their plain speaking, but Bill may have been oblivious to the deleterious effect that his words were having on his sensitive young son. So why did he choose to undermine Sellers' confidence in this way? Perhaps it was because Bill felt excluded and was resentful of the fact that, from the moment their son Peter was born, the boy appeared to occupy all his wife's waking thoughts. The possible effect of this upbringing on Sellers as an adult will be discussed shortly.

A 'nobody' with no personality?

Sikov quoted Sellers as saying, 'In myself I have nothing to offer as a personality. As far as I'm aware, I have no personality of my own, whatsoever. That is, I have no personality to offer the public. I have nothing to project.'[6]

Said Anne, 'Peter was a strange and difficult man who never really knew who he was. He buried himself in the characters he played. I remember once seeing him staring at himself in the mirror, and after a long time he said, "That's who I am – I'm just a big fat jolly boy!"'[7] This may be interpreted to mean that Sellers had no sense of self-worth. Was Sellers' fear well founded? Said Jonathan Miller of Sellers,

> He was a difficult man – sort of showbiz, sort of genius, but completely empty when he wasn't playing anyone. He was a receptacle rather than a person. And whatever parts he played completely filled the receptacle, and then they were drained out. And the receptacle was left empty and featureless. Like a lot of people who can pretend to be other people very convincingly and change their characters, he could do so because he hadn't any character himself – not unlike [actor and director Laurence] Olivier in that way.[8]

Sellers as both insecure and lonely

When asked about how he spent his spare time, Sellers replied, 'I don't mind being on my own at all.'[9] But by all accounts, this was simply not true, and he was covering up.

Milligan described Sellers as a desperately unhappy man.

> He cries for yesterday and this has made him very lonely. This constant journey is at the essence of it, like a panther in a cage, pacing backwards and forwards, for eternity. Peter's isolated. He's that lonely now. For Peter, life is just a terrible journey. He daren't stand still because he'd sink into mire of the past; he'd drown himself in his own tears, so he has to keep going although he knows he's got nowhere to go BUT, he's making the journey with all guns going and all flags flying. If there'd been a luggage compartment on Apollo 11 to the Moon, Sellers would have been in it.[10]

Following his divorce from Anne in 1963, said Michael, 'My father disliked his newly-found bachelorhood. He faced the world a lonely and forgotten man.' Also 'he instinctively feared rejection, having lost both Sophia Loren and my mother. "Who would want me?" he kept saying, as his insecurity surfaced once again. Father, always so conscious of his looks and the way he dressed, never saw himself as a heart-throb.'[11]

A feeling of being unloved

Said German actress Elke Sommer, who starred with Sellers in *A Shot in the Dark* (1964),

> Peter had something, he had this incredible sadness about him which touched me sometimes tremendously. It did not appear to me that Peter had any friends. He'd never expressed the fact that he felt loved. I think he stressed the fact that he was not loved, or he felt that he was not loved by people. He asked me to marry him despite the fact that nothing had passed between us. I think he was just desperate to marry. I always got the feeling of a very lonely man who would do practically anything to have someone who was his.[12]

It may well be, therefore, that the feeling of not being loved may also have contributed to Sellers' sense of insecurity.

Chapter 18

Sellers and Religion

To whom or to what was Sellers to turn in order to assuage the pain in his soul which Milligan and others had so identified and poignantly described? For example, was religion a comfort to him?

It seemed to Michael to be illogical that, whereas Sellers' mother Peg was Jewish and his father Bill was a Protestant, Sellers had been sent to a Catholic school. 'Dad was always puzzled by his parents' reasoning in sending him there,' he said.[1]

Said Dennis Selinger, 'Peg would go on about Peter being "a nice Jewish boy", but she had married out of the faith herself and therefore poor Peter didn't have a clue as to what he was and what he was supposed to be.' But there was a positive aspect to this, as Selinger pointed out. 'I also think it was not knowing who he was that made him so good as an actor; so he could become other characters with much more ease; so he didn't have himself to play, as opposed to say, a Gary Cooper who was always Gary Cooper.'[2] Lewis quoted him as saying, 'I'm nothing. I wasn't baptised. I wasn't bar mitzvah'd. I suppose my basic religion is doing unto others as they would do unto me.'[3]

Bar mitzvah: The religious initiation ceremony of a Jewish boy who has reached the age of 13.[4]

Walker described Sellers' 'serious discussions on religious topics' with the Reverend John Hester, Rector of Soho, London, who had 'started preparing Peter for conversion to Christianity'. However, 'He didn't stay the course of conversion.' 'He eventually felt,' said Hester, 'that if he were baptised and received into the Christian faith, he would be cutting himself off from all ties with other faiths – above all, his Jewishness.'[5]

Therefore, whatever religious views Sellers may have held, or whatever beliefs he may have adhered to, they were clearly insufficient to provide him with the comfort and reassurance that he so craved.

Chapter 19

Sellers and Superstition

Said Ian Carmichael (who was a neighbour of Sellers in Hampstead in the early 1960s), 'I got the impression that Peter was a very superstitious man.'[1] Michael pointed out, however, that such superstitions served as 'an excuse when it suited him and allowed him to misbehave.'[2]

> Superstition: a widely held but irrational belief in supernatural influences, especially as bringing good or bad luck.[3]

Said Michael,

> Most of my father's later superstitions stemmed from Peg. 'Never put keys on a table. If I give you a gift with a [sharp] point you must give me a penny. The colours green and purple are unlucky. Don't talk about the Scottish play.' [It was considered unlucky for actors to mention the name of Shakespeare's play, *Macbeth*.] All that type of thing. After Peg died, he used to burn a candle and have a picture of her by it, convinced she was present. It was probably his interest in Buddhism that prompted him to create a little shrine to his mother.[4]

Hattie Proudfoot, Sellers' personal secretary, stated that 'If you were filming and went on the set wearing something purple, that would be the end of the day. I mean, he couldn't possibly go on filming because somebody had come in wearing purple.' Said Bert Mortimer, Sellers' chauffeur and confidant, 'You should never leave a bunch of keys on the table' when Sellers was about, because 'that was bad luck'.

Said Peter Evans, 'Peter O'Toole had a superstition about green. Suddenly, after he made a film with Peter O'Toole, Peter Sellers had an obsession with the colour green.' This was a reference to the film *Casino Royale* (1967). In the film *The Prisoner of Zenda* (1979), Sellers played three parts. Said Peter Evans, 'The Mirisch brothers [the film's producers] at vast expense had this train brought from the Vienna Train Museum to the set, a big steam train, and Sellers refused to come on the set because the train was green, so they had to repaint it, and then they had to repaint it again to send it back to the Museum.' Furthermore, said Simon Williams, who appeared with Sellers both in *The Prisoner of Zenda* (1979) and *The Fiendish Plot of Dr Fu Manchu* (1980), 'We were doing a scene in the casino in Vienna and he said I can't work with these green tables, I can't have that. So, they had to go and find some blue gaming tables and during the two-day wait for the tables he said, "I just beg you Simon never to wear green, just don't wear green," and I've never been able to wear green since.'[5]

At a family reunion in Switzerland at Easter 1980, said Michael, at dinner Victoria attired herself entirely in purple. She did not know that her father had an aversion to that colour. Whereupon, Sellers declared, 'Never let me see you wearing purple again. Never, do you hear?' But when she asked her father for some money to buy some new clothes of a different colour he replied, 'As far as I'm concerned you can get the next plane and go home – I never want to see you again!'[6]

Once when on holiday in Paris, said Michael, Sellers threw away an opal ring that he had given his wife (Anne) as a present. 'A friend had told him that opals were unlucky.' On another occasion, 'I remember putting a cheese board on top of the fridge which fell heavily on Dad's head when he opened the door. He went mad and stormed through the house searching for a reason for the mishap, shouting with triumph when he found an open umbrella in the boiler room drying out after use. "Umbrellas must never be opened in the house!" he raged.'[7]

At Sellers' villa at Port Grimaud on the French Riviera, said Michael, Sellers flew into a rage and 'tossed out of the window a porcelain Gucci ashtray [which] he considered unlucky because it was embossed with a white elephant.'[8]

Simon Williams stated that his father had a superstition whereby, 'if you saw two nuns in the street, you had to walk between them.' When he mentioned this to Sellers, the response was, 'He loved that and said I'm going to try that.'

The nature of superstition

Ella Rhodes, journalist of the British Psychological Society's monthly publication *The Psychologist*, stated as follows: 'I would argue that one way to look at superstition is to think of it as an example of a cognitive illusion that makes us see causal relationships that aren't real.'[9]

> Illusion: a wrong or misinterpreted perception of a sensory experience. Causal: relating to or acting as a cause.[10]

US psychologist Stuart Vyse downplayed the significance of superstition. Said he,

> Superstition is not a sign of madness or abnormality. It is not the manifestation of serious psychological problems. Indeed, luck-enhancing superstitions may have some positive effects. Although a person is more likely to engage in superstitious behavior while experiencing certain emotions, chiefly fear and anxiety, superstition is not usually the cause of emotional difficulties.[11] The pervasive human desire for control is an important motivation for superstitious behavior. Superstitions provide a sense of control over the uncontrollable.[12]

Vyse also pointed to evidence that 'for some people, superstition serves as a method of coping with stress.'[13] This will be discussed further shortly. Vyse also used the phrase 'coincidental reinforcement'.

> Coincidence: The remarkable concurrence of events or circumstances without apparent causal connection. Coincidental: Resulting from coincidence; happening by chance. Reinforce: strengthen or support.[14]

For example,

> If a schoolchild is told that bringing charms to an examination will bring good luck, the potential for coincidental reinforcement is established. [Furthermore] A good grade is likely to encourage the

use of charms at future examinations. Even if the magic fails on the first try, other factors – such as witnessing another child's success with charms – may sustain the behavior until it is accidentally reinforced.[15]

Said Angela Haupt, Managing Editor at *US News*, 'Superstitions come from traditions and your upbringing. People teach you superstitions.' She divided superstitions into two categories: 'those that are believed to court good luck (such as having a lucky charm or pre-game ritual) and those that might help to avoid bad luck (like steering clear of a black cat on the street).'[16]

Vyse pointed to work by US psychologist Shelley Taylor, who stated that 'A sense of meaning and control can have important beneficial effects, even when they are illusions.'[17] It seems likely, therefore, that superstition has evolved as an aid to survival i.e., as a coping mechanism.

Chapter 20

Sellers and the Paranormal

From what has been said, it is clear that Sellers had a highly impressionable mind. It is hardly surprising, therefore, that he would dabble in the paranormal, as will now be seen.[1]

Clairvoyance

Clairvoyance is the supposed faculty of perceiving events in the future or beyond normal sensory contact.[2]

Maurice Woodruff was a well-known clairvoyant of his day. Sellers first met him in 1959. Even when Sellers was abroad, said Bert Mortimer, his chauffeur and confidant, he kept in touch with a clairvoyant.[3] Said actress Katie Boyle, a friend of Sellers, 'I wasn't enamoured of the gentleman. I always felt that he found out about his subjects before he met them and therefore could talk about them rather freely.' When the film producers got to hear about this, said Peter Evans, they would try to influence Woodruff to point Sellers in the right direction and say, 'There's a couple of bob in it for you.'[4] Dennis Selinger (Sellers' agent) stated that Woodruff was in the habit of telephoning him and asking his advice as to what he ought to say to Sellers in respect of the current film project in hand. Of this, Sellers himself was quite unaware.[5] Said Carmichael, 'I used to see Peter's car outside Maurice's house frequently and I understood, at that sort of time, that Peter would rarely make a major decision about his career without first going and consulting Maurice Woodruff.'[6]

Yoga

In the 1960s, said Roger Lewis, Sellers 'tried everything and he was into all that long hair and beads and the Beatles and all that George Harrison stuff.'

George Harrison, musician and lead guitarist of the Beatles, spoke of the time when Sellers 'actually became a hippy around the late 60s', and with Indian musician and composer Ravi Shankar, they 'hung out together. He knew that there was something else in life but the sad thing about Peter was that I don't think he was on the road to that. You know, he was doing yoga, he was trying to hone in on "Who am I? What is it all about?"'[7]

Hippies were part of a subculture which rejected traditional social values, advocated peace and free love, and favoured long hair and unconventional dress.[8]

Michael was extremely cynical. 'I saw most of those guys as charlatans,' he said, 'much the same as Maurice Woodruff with different clothes on, same rubbish, different flare.'[9]

In the early 1970s, Sellers took up yoga and obtained all the accoutrements including 'a statue of Buddha, incense, and a porcelain three-headed elephant symbolizing the Eastern gods.'

Yoga is a Hindu spiritual and ascetic discipline, a part of which, including breath control, simple meditation, and the adoption of specific bodily postures, is widely practised in the West for health and relaxation.[10] Ascetic behaviour is characterised by severe self-discipline and abstention from all forms of indulgence, typically for religious reasons.[11]

However, said Michael 'his yoga days were numbered' and 'soon the altar, the kaftans and velvet prayer cushions disappeared without trace from his house, as though they had never existed.'[12]

The supernatural

The supernatural is defined as a manifestation or event attributed to some force beyond scientific understanding or the laws of nature.[13]

When Sellers was cast as Evelyn Tremble, one of several agents pretending to be James Bond in the film *Casino Royale* (1967), Orson Welles was invited to join the cast. But, said Peter Evans, Welles was a superb conjurer and Sellers, 'was terrified that Orson would use his magical powers to destroy his performance if not himself. He became obsessed with this.'[14]

> Magic: the power of apparently influencing events by using mysterious or supernatural forces.[15]

Said Sellers' biographer Peter Evans,

> On one occasion he said to me, 'Have you ever looked at yourself in the mirror: really looked at yourself for a long, long time.' I said, 'How long?' 'Two hours,' he said. I said, 'No, I've never done two hours, looking at myself.' So he said, 'Well I have. Peg [his mother] used to say no, I mustn't do it I've got to stop doing it because I'll see the devil if I go on looking.' I said, 'Well, have you ever found the devil?' 'Oh yes,' he said. 'Oh yes.'[16]

Astrology

Sellers developed an interest in astrology, which is defined as the study of the movement and relative positions of celestial bodies interpreted as having an influence on human affairs and the natural world.[17] Said Scottish film director Joe McGrath, director of *Casino Royale* (1967), 'I know that he did spend a lot of time and money getting daily horoscopes. A lot of his intimates, his agents and secretaries were sent off to get the latest document [presumably newspapers or magazine] each day to tell him how to organise his day.'[18]

A horoscope is a forecast of a person's future based on the relative positions of the stars and planets at the time of their birth.[19] Of course, as with any other superstition, coincidental reinforcement, as described above, would have occurred whenever astrological predictions came true.

'Psychic surgeons'

In the summer of 1978, said Michael, Sellers consulted 'a group of psychic surgeons' in the Philippines, 'who claimed miracle cures even for cases regarded as terminal.' This was despite the showing of a British TV documentary which had exposed these surgeons as 'tricksters whose practices were condemned throughout the medical profession.'[20]

> Psychic: relating to or denoting faculties or phenomena that are apparently inexplicable by natural laws, especially those involving telepathy or clairvoyance. Telepathy: the supposed communication of thoughts by means other than the known senses.[21]

Did Sellers find such practices helpful to his sense of mental well-being? Perhaps, but if so, the effect was only temporary, as will be seen.

Chapter 21

Sellers and Spiritualism

Said Peter Evans, Sellers 'was deeply impressed by Michael Bentine [comedian and founder member of the Goons], and Bentine was probably the first person to put the idea into Sellers' head that there was something here, something worth checking out.'[1] Said Milligan of Bentine, 'He was an extraordinary character who told me the most extraordinary stories. He once told me that his mother had levitated from the ground, across the dining room table and settled on the other side.'[2]

Spiritualism is defined as the system of belief or religious practice based on supposed communication with the spirits of the dead, especially through mediums. Mediums claim to be able to communicate between the dead and the living.[3]

When Peter Sellers married Britt Ekland in February 1964 and they set up home in Los Angeles, he continued to attend seances, as he had previously done in England.[4]

> Séance: a meeting at which people attempt to make contact with the dead.[5]

Said Dennis Selinger of Sellers' mother Peg, 'After she had gone [i.e. died on 30 January 1967], he used to have conversations with her. He would go into a room and talk to her for quite some time.'[6] And of course, whenever Sellers believed that he had actually made contact with his late mother, this would have led to a reinforcement of his beliefs.

In the film *The Magic Christian* (released in the UK in December 1969), Sellers played the part of eccentric billionaire, Sir Guy Grand. One day during the filming, Sellers was in his dressing room when he summoned Joe McGrath, the film's director. 'He was sitting dressed as a nun,' said Evans. 'He was looking in the mirror and he said, "Who is it? Who is it, Joe?"' Whereupon, he answered his own question by saying, 'Yes, that's my mum.' Perhaps, in some macabre way, Sellers was trying to bring his mother back to life.[7]

From March 1971 to spring 1972, when Sellers lived in Ireland with his third wife Miranda Quarry, he invited spiritualist Estelle Roberts from London to visit him. Said Evans,

> she introduced him to her spirit guide called 'Red Cloud'" who was an Indian Chief [Native American]. Peter was very impressed with this, I mean, the drama of an Indian Chief and spirit guide was bound to absolutely captivate him in his imagination. He came with a full Indian costume complete with feathered head dress. Red Cloud said that Peter's spirit guide was a late Victorian music hall star called Dan Leno. Peter immediately asked me what I could find out about Dan Leno, which I duly did.[8]

Dan Leno (1860–1904, real name George Wild Galvin) was a leading English music hall comedian and actor of the late Victorian and early Edwardian eras.

Said Mortimer, Sellers 'felt that Dan Leno gave him the inspiration. He came inside him. He said Dan Leno was working him, gave him his talent.'[9]

Said Evans,

> I went over to Ireland to see him [Sellers] and he said, 'I don't know what I'm going to do but Dan Leno thinks I should do these *Pink Panther* films.' I said, 'But when did you last talk to Dan?' 'Well,' he said, 'he's coming over all the time. He's very insistent about it. I've got to listen to Dan you know.' Now that's either a conversation with a madman or a conversation with someone who genuinely deeply believes that Dan Leno who died in 1910 [in fact, in 1904] or thereabouts has gone to Ireland to advise him to play a crazy detective in a Hollywood movie.

But in retrospect, judging by the enormous success of the film, said Evans, 'the fact is Dan was right!'[10]

Referring to Sellers' sessions with medium Estelle Roberts, said Walker, the experience it gave Sellers of contacting the deceased became very relevant indeed to his film-making and eventually central to his life. The uncanny feeling that the medium was 'possessed', by those wanting to make their presences felt from 'the other side', helped Sellers define his own curious and rather frightened reaction to the characters he created. He came to see himself as a medium, as if the film characters had entered his body, transfusing his personality so powerfully with their own that they took him over. From that it was to be just a short jump in credulity to the point where he convinced himself that these were not simply fictitious characters, the offspring of some screen writer's imagination. They were lives that he himself, whomever *he* might be, had lived at other times, in other places, under other names. Acting, in short, was a process of past-life recall.[11]

Said Blake Edwards, 'I think had he not been Peter Sellers he very likely could have been in a government institution [i.e. a psychiatric hospital].' For example, '3 o'clock in the morning the phone would ring. I wake up. He'd say, "Blake, this is Peter. I've just talked to God and he told me how to do the scene tomorrow." But he wasn't joking. He had just talked to God.' Also, Sellers 'used to carry a shrine around with him. He talked to his mother all the time, his deceased mother.'[12]

One day when he did that to me, I walked on the set the next day and said, 'Well, what did he tell you to do?' And he said, 'We'll just leave the camera where it was, and I'll show you.' And so, we rolled the camera and he showed me, and came over with a big smile on his face and said, 'What do you think?' And I said, 'Do me a favour. Ask God not to call any more. Get out of show business,' which he didn't like, and he left, and we didn't see him for the rest of the day. He really was quite mad. Some of the best times I had in my life were with Peter, and the worst, absolutely the worst![13]

Said Vyse, 'Many people accept the validity of ESP and communication with the dead.'

ESP: Extrasensory perception: the supposed faculty of perceiving things by means other than the known senses, e.g. by telepathy.)[14]

'If you actually employ these ideas in your life – for example, to communicate with your deceased grandmother – then by our definition these occult beliefs would be superstitious.'[15]

In other words, Vyse regarded belief in the occult (supernatural or magical powers, practices, or phenomena[16]) as a superstition.

Sellers' idiosyncratic beliefs, and behaviour on account of those beliefs was, in the main, harmless, if somewhat disconcerting to his family, friends, and acquaintances. But can this be classed as a mental disorder or illness?

Chapter 22

Was Sellers Insane? A Personality Disorder?

Over the years, many people opined as to the nature of Sellers' mental state. Said comedy writer Denis Norden of Sellers, 'My perception of him as a man was that he was utterly untrustworthy and entirely loveable: you couldn't put your money on him for anything. Then there was this sort of manic depressive thing, which he shared with a lot of great comedians. He was a good mate.'[1]

Bipolar disorder (formerly known as manic depression) is characterised by 'major depressive episodes' during the course of life and 'serious impairment in work and social functioning'. Admittedly, Sellers did experience depression, but usually for good reason, and therefore as far as he is concerned, this diagnosis can be ruled out.

Film critic Barry Norman described Sellers' 'general lunacy. In his own way he was touched with genius but also in his own way he was touched with madness.'[2]

Blake Edwards, in an interview, agreed that Peter Sellers was a comic and a genius, but said that he had his dark side. 'Crazy, certifiable,' said Edwards of Sellers.[3]

'Lunacy', 'madness', and 'craziness' are non-specific terms and are therefore not helpful in this context.

Simon Williams described Sellers as 'a bit off the wall', 'a bit flaky', and 'as mad as a fucking snake.' However, this is not a helpful metaphor for two reasons; firstly, snakes are rational creatures in the main, and secondly, it goes no way to explaining Sellers' mindset.[4] So, where did the truth lie?

A personality disorder is defined as 'an enduring pattern of inner experience and behaviour that deviates markedly from the expectations of the individual's culture, is pervasive and inflexible, has an onset in early adolescence or early adulthood, is stable over time, and leads to distress and impairment.'[5]

Psychiatrists tend to classify personality disorders as 'paranoid', 'schizoid', 'schizotypal', 'antisocial', etc., but the truth is that each and every person is an individual and there is often a considerable overlap between one group and another.

> Psychiatrist: A medical practitioner specialising in the diagnosis and treatment of mental illness. Psychiatry: The branch of medicine concerned with the study and treatment of mental illness, emotional disturbance, and abnormal behaviour.[6]

Furthermore, the very phrase 'personality disorder' may be seen as pejorative, in that many features of such 'disorders' may be viewed as occupying different ends of the normal spectrum.

> Pejorative: expressing contempt or disapproval.[7]

Therefore, instead of 'personality disorder', 'personality variation' or 'eccentricity', might be considered to be more appropriate and kinder terms. The question is, where, if anywhere, does Peter Sellers fit into this spectrum of so-called personality disorders?

According to the *Diagnostic and Statistical Manual of Mental Disorders*,[8] the following types of personality disorder are characterised by the following features. Furthermore, those features which apply particularly to Peter Sellers, and have been revealed in the above narrative, are shown in bold.

Schizotypal Personality Disorder (SPD)

A schizotype is defined as a personality type in which mild symptoms of schizophrenia are present.

> Schizophrenia: a long-term mental disorder of a type involving a breakdown in the relationship between thought, emotion, and behaviour, leading to faulty perception, inappropriate actions and feelings, and withdrawal from reality into fantasy and delusion.[9]

Individuals with SPD may exhibit the following characteristics:

Ideas of reference (i.e., incorrect interpretations of casual incidents and external events as having a particular and unusual meaning specifically for the person). These individuals may be superstitious or preoccupied with paranormal phenomena that are outside the norms of their subculture. **Odd beliefs or magical thinking that influences behavior and is inconsistent with subcultural norms (e.g. superstition, belief in clairvoyance, telepathy, or 'sixth sense'). Unusual perceptual experiences, including bodily illusions.** ... They may feel that they have special powers to sense events before they happen or to read others' thoughts. They may believe that they have magical control over others, which can be implemented directly or indirectly through compliance with magical rituals. **Perceptual alterations may be present (e.g. sensing that another person is present or hearing a voice murmuring his or her name)** ... Individuals with this disorder are often suspicious and may have paranoid ideation.

Ideate: imagine.

Paranoia: a mental condition characterised by delusions of persecution, unwarranted jealousy, or exaggerated self-importance: unjustified suspicion and mistrust of others.[10]

Individuals with SPD experience interpersonal relatedness as problematic and are uncomfortable relating to other people. Although they may express unhappiness about their lack of relationships, their behavior suggests a decreased desire for intimate contact. As a result, they usually have no or few close friends or confidants other than a first-degree relative. **They are anxious in social situations, particularly those involving unfamiliar people.** They will interact with other individuals when they have to but prefer to keep to themselves because they feel that they are different and just do not 'fit in'. Their social anxiety does not easily abate, even when they spend more time in the setting or become more familiar with the other people, because their anxiety tends to be associated with suspiciousness regarding others' motivations.[11]

Borderline Personality Disorder (BPD)

'The essential feature of BPD is a pervasive pattern of instability of interpersonal relationships, self-image, and affects, and marked impulsivity.'

Affect: emotion or desire as influencing behaviour.[12]

Individuals with BPD make frantic efforts to avoid real or imagined abandonment. The perception of impending separation or rejection, or the loss of external structure, can lead to profound changes in self-image, affect, cognition, and behavior.

Cognition: the mental action or process of acquiring knowledge through thought, experience, and the senses.[13]

These individuals are very sensitive to environmental circumstances. They experience intense abandonment fears and inappropriate anger even when faced with a realistic time-limited separation or when there are unavoidable changes in plans. They may believe that this 'abandonment' implies that they are 'bad'... These abandonment fears are related to an intolerance of being alone and a need to have other people with them. Their frantic efforts to avoid abandonment may include impulsive actions such as self-mutilating or suicidal behaviors.

Individuals with BPD have a pattern of unstable and intense relationships. They may idealize potential caregivers or lovers at the first or second meeting, demand to spend a lot of time together, and share the most intimate details early in a relationship. However, they may switch quickly from idealizing other people to devaluing them, feeling that the other person does not care enough, does not give enough, or is not 'there' enough. These individuals can empathize with and nurture other people, but only with the expectation that the other person will 'be there' in return to meet their own needs on demand.

These individuals are prone to sudden and dramatic shifts in their view of others, who may alternatively be seen as beneficent supports or as cruelly punitive. Such shifts often reflect disillusionment with a caregiver whose nurturing qualities have been idealized or whose rejection or abandonment is expected.

There may be an identity disturbance characterised by markedly and persistently unstable self-image or sense of self. There are sudden and dramatic shifts in self-image, characterized by shifting goals, values, and vocational aspirations. There may be sudden changes in opinions and plans about career, sexual identity, values, and types of friends.

These individuals may suddenly change from the role of a needy supplicant for help to that of a righteous avenger of past mistreatment. Although they usually have a self-image that is based on being bad or evil, individuals with this disorder may at times have feelings that they do not exist at all. Such experiences usually occur in situations in which the individual feels a lack of meaningful relationship, nurturing, and support.

Individuals with BPD display impulsivity in ... areas that are potentially self-damaging. They may gamble, spend money irresponsibly, binge eat, abuse substances, engage in unsafe sex, or drive recklessly. Individuals with this disorder display recurrent suicidal behavior, gestures, or threats, or self-mutilating behavior. These self-destructive acts are usually precipitated by threats of separation or rejection.

Individuals with BPD may display affective instability that is due to a marked reactivity of mood. **The basic dysphoric mood of those with BPD is often disrupted by periods of anger, panic, or despair and is rarely relieved by periods of well-being or satisfaction.**

Dysphoria: a state of unease or general dissatisfaction.[14]

These episodes may reflect the individual's extreme reactivity to interpersonal stresses. **Individuals with BPD may be troubled by chronic feelings of emptiness. Easily bored, they may constantly seek something to do. Individuals with this disorder frequently express inappropriate, intense anger or have difficulty controlling their anger. They may display extreme sarcasm, enduring bitterness, or verbal outbursts. The anger is often elicited when a caregiver or** lover is seen as neglectful, withholding, uncaring, or abandoning. Such expressions of anger are often followed by shame and guilt and contribute to the feeling that they have of being evil. During periods of extreme stress, transient paranoid ideation or dissociative symptoms may occur.

Dissociation: separation of normally related mental processes, resulting in one group functioning independently from the rest and leading to disorders such as multiple personality.[15]

'The real or perceived return of the caregiver's nurturance may result in a remission of symptoms.'[16]

Histrionic Personality Disorder (HPD)

The essential feature of HPD is pervasive and excessive emotionality and attention-seeking behavior. Individuals with HPD are uncomfortable or feel unappreciated when they are not the center of attention. Often lively and dramatic, they tend to draw attention to themselves and may initially charm new acquaintances by their enthusiasm, apparent openness, or flirtatiousness. These qualities wear thin, however, as these individuals continually demand to be the center of attention. If they are not the center of attention, they may do something dramatic (e.g. make up stories, create a scene) to draw the focus of attention to themselves. They may 'fish for compliments' regarding appearance and may be easily and excessively upset by critical comment about how they look or by a photograph that they regard as unflattering.[17]

Avoidant Personality Disorder (APD)

The essential feature of APD is pervasive pattern of social inhibition, feelings of inadequacy, and hypersensitivity to negative evaluation. These individuals avoid making new friends unless they are certain they will be liked and accepted without criticism. Unless they pass stringent tests proving the contrary, other people are assumed to be critical and disapproving.

Individuals with this disorder will not join in group activities unless there are repeated and generous offers of support and nurturance. Interpersonal intimacy is often difficult for these individuals, although they are able to establish intimate relationships when there is assurance of uncritical acceptance. Because individuals with this disorder are preoccupied with being criticised or rejected in social situations, they may have a markedly low threshold for detecting such reactions. If someone is even slightly disapproving or critical, they may feel extremely hurt. They tend to be shy, quiet, inhibited, and 'invisible' because of the fear that any attention would be degrading or rejecting.

These individuals believe themselves to be socially inept, personally unappealing, or inferior to others.[18]

Dependent Personality Disorder (DPD)

The essential feature of DPD is a pervasive and excessive need to be taken care of that leads to submissive and clinging behavior and fears of separation. The dependent and submissive behaviors are designed to elicit caregiving and arise from self-perception of being unable to function adequately without help of others. When a close relationship ends (e.g. a breakup with a lover; the death of a caregiver), individuals with DPD may urgently seek another relationship to provide the care and support they need.

Their belief that they are unable to function in the absence of a close relationship motivates these individuals to become quickly and indiscriminately attached to another individual.

Individuals with this disorder are often preoccupied with fears of being left to care for themselves. They see themselves as so totally dependent on the advice and help of an important other person that they worry about being abandoned by that person when there are no grounds to justify such fears.[19]

Paranoid Personality Disorder (PPD)

The essential feature of PPD is a pattern of pervasive mistrust and suspiciousness of others such that their motives are interpreted as

malevolent. Individuals with this disorder persistently bear grudges and are unwilling to forgive the insults, injuries, or slights that they think they have received. They may blame others for their own shortcomings.[20]

Antisocial Personality Disorder (ASPD)

'The essential feature of ASPD is a pervasive pattern of disregard for, and violation of, the rights of others.' An associated feature is 'lack of empathy'.[21]

Conclusion

There must be hardly a person in the world who doesn't display one or more of the above characteristics. Sellers, however, had characteristics in abundance in each of the categories named above!

A point of great significance is that all the different personality disorders outlined above which relate to Sellers *have their onset in early adulthood.* This, of course, explains something which Sellers' children Michael and Sarah, and their mother Anne (and undoubtedly Victoria and her mother Britt), puzzled over and were deeply perplexed by: why Sellers changed from being a loving father to one who was often ambivalent about the welfare of his wives and children, and downright cruel to them at times. It also explains the adult Sellers' often bizarre behaviour towards friends, acquaintances, work associates, etc, though those in his inner circle such as the Goons were spared the worst excesses of it.

Chapter 23

Possible Origins of Sellers' Personality Disorder

Childhood emotional abuse

Sellers stated that his father Bill had repeatedly told him as a child that he would finish up as a road sweeper. Whether his father said this in a light-hearted way, or whether it was said in all seriousness, is not known. However, if the latter was the case, this does not necessarily imply maliciousness on Bill's part. It may simply have reflected his anxiety as to whether his son would 'make good'. But in speaking in this way he may have failed to understand the sensitive nature and vulnerability of his son. To all intents and purposes, it did amount to a degree of childhood emotional abuse, however unintentional it may have been on Bill's part.

In his book *Child Care and the Growth of Love*, US psychiatrist John Bowlby explained how 'the quality of the parental care which a child receives in his [or her] earliest years is of vital importance for his future mental health.'[1] Said Bowlby,

> what is believed to be essential for mental health is that an infant and young child should experience a warm, intimate, and continuous relationship with his mother (or permanent mother-substitute – one person who steadily 'mothers him') in which both find satisfaction and enjoyment. It is this complex, rich, and rewarding relationship with the mother in early years, varied in countless ways by relations with the father and with the brothers and sisters, that child psychiatrists and many others now believe to underlie the development of character and of mental health.[2]

In other words, although Bowlby stresses the important role of the mother, he acknowledges that the role of the father is also crucial.

However, said Bowlby, 'it is by no means clear why some children are damaged' by 'the deprivation of mother-love in early childhood ... and some are not.'[3] This may depend on the resilience of the particular child in question. Sellers, however, was not an emotionally resilient person.

Community scientist Tamara Taillieu and her colleagues from the University of Manitoba, Canada, concluded that although emotional maltreatment was 'a difficult construct to define and measure', nevertheless childhood emotional maltreatment was associated with 'increased odds of lifetime diagnoses' of several mental disorders. The crux of the matter was the nature of the attachment bond which the child forms with its parents.

> Once an attachment pattern is formed, it tends to persist and influences an individual's perception of self and others throughout the lifespan. Emotional maltreatment likely interferes with the development of a secure attachment bond, and the consequent insecure attachment patterns could help to explain the association between childhood emotional maltreatment and mental disorders.[4]

Emotional maltreatment, said US paediatricians Steven W. Kairys and Charles F. Johnson, 'destroys a child's sense of self and personal security'.[5]

Such emotional abuse, said Taillieu et al., included parental 'belittling', 'degradation', and 'hostility'. 'Emotional abuse may be particularly harmful to long-term mental health because negative cognitions are directly given to the child (e.g. you are worthless).'

> Cognition: The mental action or process of acquiring knowledge through thought, experience, and the senses.[6]

The authors listed the resultant personality disorders as follows: Paranoid; Schizotypal; Antisocial; Borderline; Avoidant; Dependent, all of which have been previously mentioned in relation to Sellers. In addition, the authors mention Schizoid (lack of interest or detachment from social relationships, apathy, restricted emotional expression); Histrionic (excessive attention seeking, excessive emotions); Narcissistic (feelings of grandiosity, arrogance, excessive need for praise, lack of empathy); Grandiose (impressive or magnificent, especially pretentiously[7]);

Obsessive-compulsive (rigid conformity to rules, perfectionism, excessive orderliness). However, none of the latter disorders appear to relate typically to Sellers.[8]

To conclude, perhaps Bill Sellers did use the term 'road sweeper' in a light-hearted manner in respect of his son. And even if the remarks were made abusively, some might argue that the youth had more than sufficient support from his doting mother to compensate for this. Nonetheless, if Sellers was an ultrasensitive child, as seems likely to have been the case, he may have taken his father's comments to heart and attached undue importance to them, with the possible outcome as described above.

Drug abuse

Drug taking is a culture among many celebrities, and Sellers was no exception. To him, this probably provided another form of escapism from the trauma and stresses of the real world.

When she first met Sellers in February 1964, said Britt, he offered her marijuana (cannabis) and told her to inhale and hold her breath for as long as she could. 'We all smoked in the sixties,' she said.[9]

'When I was 13,' said Michael, i.e. in 1967, 'like most of my chums in the class, I was smoking pot. It was easy to get. Dad was smoking it too, and he kept the grass in empty film canisters in the house ... There was so much of the stuff that I knew he wouldn't miss a little. It was like his pills – he had thousands of them – and I would help myself to amphetamines [stimulants] or Mandrax [methaqualone] sleeping pills.'[10]

('Pot' and 'grass' are alternative names for cannabis.)

In March 1971, Sellers moved to Ireland with his third wife, Miranda Quarry. 'By that time,' said Roger Lewis, 'he was pretty far gone on marijuana most of the time. I think he wasn't in his right mind when he was in Ireland – whatever his right mind was like anyway.'[11]

It was in the early 1970s, when Miranda and Sellers were in Paris together, said Michael, that his father first 'dabbled in "acid" [the hallucinogenic drug LSD]'. However, 'he had a bad trip,' and vowed that 'he would never touch LSD again'.[12]

Michael referred to the time, in the late 1970s, when his half-sister Victoria 'discovered Dad's hidden supplies of dope'. ('Dope' usually refers to cannabis or heroin.) When her mother Britt got to hear of it, she 'threatened to have Victoria arrested if she was ever caught smoking pot at home'.[13] By this time, Sellers was an amphetamine addict.[14]

On 19 July 1980, five days before his death, Sellers checked in at the Dorchester Hotel. And when he and his father were having dinner together, said Michael, 'Dad produced a joint [a cannabis cigarette] and lit it, and was about to hand it on to me but then remembered I'd given up smoking. It worried me that he was still drinking and taking drugs when it was clear that his health was in a bad state.'[15]

Did any of the above drugs have psychotropic effects, and if so, could they explain Sellers' personality disorder?

> Psychotropic: referring to drugs that affect a person's mental state.[16]

LSD can be discounted, as Sellers had an immediate adverse reaction to it. So also can Mandrax. With amphetamines, psychoses such as delusions and paranoia can occur but only with large doses. Cannabis, in addition to inducing a state of relaxation and euphoria, may also cause cognitive impairment. It has also been implicated in triggering latent psychoses, but not actually being the source of them. Finally, these symptoms are present during drug intoxication and drug withdrawal but disappear in between times.[17] Given that Sellers' personality disorder was a permanent feature of his make-up, it is therefore unlikely that drugs were the cause of it.

An inherited, genetically based disorder

In 2010, Ted Reichborn-Kjennerud stated as follows: 'Genetic epidemiological studies indicate that all ten personality disorders classified on the DSM-IV axis II are modestly to moderately heritable. Shared environmental and nonadditive genetic factors are of minor or no importance.'[18]

> Axis: Domain whereby five axes each relate to a different aspect of mental disorder. Nonadditive: where the value is less than the sum of values for the component parts.

It therefore appears likely that Sellers' personality disorder was inherited. This begs the question, from whom? Was there anyone else in the family with such a disorder? In this respect, his parents would be the first port of call. Peg was highly superstitious, this being a feature of Schizotypal Personality Disorder. She was also extremely possessive (in respect of her son), this being a feature of Borderline Personality Disorder. As for Bill, he was probably the source of 'fake news' in respect of his over-exaggerated and often blatantly false alleged past achievements, and having a grandiose image of oneself is a feature of Narcissistic Personality Disorder.

Chapter 24

A Rollercoaster of Joy and Despair

The good days…

When Sellers was asked by Milligan what were his happiest days, when did he have the most fun, he replied that they were Sundays when he was performing in *The Goon Show*. 'I used to live for those Sundays,' said Sellers. 'All our ideas and thoughts went into the show, everything we had. We were just so keen to let people hear what was going into our minds. It was just so crazy.'[1] Sellers once told Milligan that 'he was never happier than when doing *The Goon Shows*.'[2] Secombe agreed. The time that 'we all loved best', he said, was when the Goons got together for a rehearsal, and 'Peter and I would fall around giggling as we read the script for the first time. Spike would watch anxiously for our reactions to his efforts before joining in the general laughter.'[3] If ever anyone doubted whether Peter Sellers was capable of bonding with friends and enjoying life to the full, they should watch recordings of rehearsals of *The Goon Show*, where the four 'Goons' would wrestle on the floor together and romp about.[4]

Amongst the guests at the Sellers' home Brookfield, Elstead, Surrey in the mid-to-late 1960s, said Bert Mortimer, was Prince Charles. This was because the Prince 'was a great admirer of the Goons'. Furthermore, usually the meetings would be at Prince Charles' instigation. So, 'Sellers got together Harry Secombe and Spike Milligan and they all had this wonderful lunch where there were guffaws of laughter coming from the house and Prince Charles used to actually do the voices. He was very, very good at it.'[5]

When, in April 1960, Sellers arrived in New York City for a two-week tour to promote the films *The Battle of the Sexes* and *I'm All Right Jack*, which were currently playing on Broadway, he was delighted to hear *The Goon Show* and the Goons' signature song 'Ying tong iddle I po' being broadcast on local radio.[6]

In respect of his acting career, Sellers told Parkinson that

> the only time that you're really happy is a time when you're doing the take; not when the film is out, not when you're preparing for the film, the moment you're doing the take on the floor. And when you do it, and that moment comes out of you and you've done it, you remember that, and that's the time when the full feeling of achievement comes out.[7]

Which character had Sellers enjoyed playing the most? Interviewed by Steve Allen on the *Steve Allen Show* in Hollywood in 1964, he declared with a broad smile, 'I think I enjoyed playing Dr Strangelove the most.'[8]

Sellers also confessed that he had been truly happy when on his boat at sea. That was the ultimate luxury for him. There was nobody there, and the crew didn't bother him unnecessarily.[9] But he issued a caveat. Whatever happiness he had experienced, he said, had occurred only fleetingly. 'If you had happiness all the time,' he said, 'you'd probably get blasé with it. You'd never appreciate it when it came along.' He confessed that, having achieved his aims he was 'very happy. Two lovely children [he would go on to have a third child, Victoria, by second wife Britt Ekland], wonderful children, and when I'm with them it's marvellous, everything's great, but the periods when I'm on my own, it's not so great.'[10]

Said Peter Evans, 'We were talking about his life and I said, "You're rich, you're successful, you should be happy now." He said, "No. The only time he had been really happy was when he lived in Hampstead with his first wife Anne." Sellers described the beautiful view from the window of their apartment and said, "I could almost see the past then." And that was the kind of the nearest I think he ever got to admitting that, may be that was it, that things were closing in on him.'[11]

And the bad...

As a result of his divorce from Anne in 1963, said Michael, his father 'felt drained of his talent to act; there was no limit to the depths of his melancholy.'[12] When Sellers attended their daughter Sarah's birthday party, soon after Anne had remarried in that same year, Anne said of her former husband, '"You are probably the saddest person I know." He had everything he'd ever wanted professionally and financially, yet he had nothing – not even his children.'[13]

Sometimes Sellers felt so suicidal that Bert Mortimer, David Lodge, and Bill Kerr stayed up with him during the night on 'suicide watch'. When Mortimer asked him if he'd ever thought of going to see a psychiatrist, Sellers replied, 'out of the depths of his misery, "psychiatrists only talk common sense to you".'[14]

Said Mortimer, Sellers 'liked people around him whom he knew, whom he felt confident with. And he had a great time. But then, all of a sudden for no reason, he'd enter into a depression again. He was a very complex character altogether.'[15]

Perhaps the most insightful picture of Sellers was given by his friend Milligan who, in 1969, reappraised Sellers' life to date.

> He's 44 now, and a long way from Southsea where he was born; a long way too from touring round in his parents' Ford [motor car], the RAF, and India, and in Germany, six weeks at the old *Windmill*, seven years of *The Goon Shows*, thirty-eight films in just over ten years, divorced twice, three children, plays, pantomimes the lot and yet it's all come to nothing.[16]

In 1974, Sellers received some bad news about his financial investments. Said Mortimer,

> he hadn't shaved himself for several days, but he had cut off a lot of his hair, in a very rough, uneven fashion. Some of it was quite short, other parts he had left long and straggling so that it looked as if he had gone bald in a very patchy fashion. He didn't give us any reason why he'd done this. 'I was just so depressed,' he kept on saying.[17]

This action by Sellers amounts to self-mutilation, which as already mentioned is a feature of Borderline Personality Disorder.
Said Blake Edwards,

> When you get as complicated as Peter was it's really hard to diagnose him or analyse him. He was not a happy man. He had happy times, which I think were well overshadowed by his demons. I think that

he lived most of his life in hell. I think most comic actors are not very happy people. Difficult [for him] to live on this planet? Yes, I think it was very difficult.[18]

This was the case even in Sellers' later life when, said Michael,

I saw an unhappy, used up man. He was old before his time. Why? Because of the illness, and the drugs he had to take just to keep alive. And you can actually see that in the Fu Manchu film he made, especially the 'Nayland Smith' character. The face is really thin and hollow, all the fat's gone out of his flesh. I was sad for him in a way. There was a man who had everything. He'd been there and done that and couldn't see that there was anything more, and he was used up and it was quite sad.[19]

Chapter 25

Why Sellers Could Not Be Happy for Any Length of Time

Said Michael, 'with all the stardom and riches secured, Dad could never find real happiness. Not in the mansions, the limousine and yachts he came to buy. Not among the members of the Royal Family and aristocracy he was to brush shoulders with. Nor could he find lasting contentment with any of his future wives.'[1] Said Sellers himself, 'I like to be happy, yes, I like to be happy very much. You could say, right, successful; *Being There*; three beautiful children; my health; all these material things round me. Why aren't you happy?'[2] This is a tacit admission by Sellers that he was unhappy. But why?

Sellers' innate pessimism

Said Peter Evans,

> Sellers was never sure about himself. He was never convinced that good things were going to happen. He was always convinced that bad things were going to happen, so he needed somebody in his life to tell him he was great and once he got that assurance, he kind of fulfilled the prophecy.[3] When he was married to Anne, his first wife, she kept control of that kind of danger in his life, but when he started to get really successful, he divorced Anne and the control over him began to slip away. He was on his own and that was madness.[4]

Sellers as being constantly bored and dissatisfied

Said Sarah Sellers, once her father became rich and famous and there was nobody to say 'No' to him,

I think he found it really hard to come to terms with his relationships, and he was in a position that he felt he could put them to one side and go on to the next. It wasn't just women in his life. That was how he operated. You know, once he got bored with one toy it was on to the next. It was a constant quest and I think the women were really just part of that.[5]

Wherever Sellers went, said Milligan, it was

boring. Can you imagine the agony of it? If he hadn't made it financially, he'd have killed himself. This was the 'terrible crucifix' he had to bear. For Peter, life is just a terrible journey. He can't stand still because he'd sink in the mire of his past, so he has to keep going even though he knows he's got nowhere to go. Peter tired even of the boat [the *Victoria Maria*], like everything else in his life, when faced with the reality of something. He had no choice but to run away, the yacht, his home, all a dream.[6]

Was marriage or female company the answer?

Said Milligan of Britt, Sellers' second wife,

he married [her] eleven days after he met her. No wonder it didn't last, people said. But it wasn't that at all. He wanted the security his mother had given him and so, naturally he thought it must come through marriage. He was always trying to replace the security of his home and his mother and that security was a dream, it bore no relation to the real world. When he went out into the world and got married, everyone was trying to take him for what they could get. The world is full of obligations and liabilities. To him the world seemed like a violent attack upon his warm, glowing, mother/son relationship and it cracked him to pieces.[7]

Said Sellers himself, in a rare moment of candidness,

I feel extremely vulnerable and that I need help a lot, a lot. I suppose I feel mainly that I need the help of a woman, so I am continually searching for this woman. I keep reading of these great women behind men, who support them and push them forward and they mother you. They're great in bed, they're like a sister, they're not there when you don't want to see them, and they are there when you want to see them. I don't know where they are. Maybe they are around somewhere. I'll find one, one of these days.[8]

But when asked by Parkinson, 'Are you going to find the kind of fulfilment you're looking for in your work or in a relationship with a woman?' Sellers replied, 'I don't think I'll ever find it in a relationship with a woman.'[9] In respect of Sellers' marriages, said Forbes, he was 'seeking the perfect bluebird of happiness that sadly always eluded him'.[10]

Sellers' late mother Peg, as being someone irreplaceable

Said Milligan, Sellers 'could never be happily married because the person on whom he most depended was dead', i.e. Peg.

> He was an only child and his mother Peg naturally wanted him to have the very best in life but she didn't have the best in life to give him; so she sacrificed her responsibilities to her husband and made Peter head of the household. Any time of the day or night he would call her. "Peg", "Peg", and she would drop everything and come round immediately, so what he lost was the perfect set up, except that this boy never really got over it.[11]

Sellers described how, 'when my mother died, although I had children alive, she was my last close relative. I felt a great feeling of loneliness. I just couldn't pick up the phone and speak to my mother anymore. I felt that a lot.'[12] Anyone who has lost their mother will identify wholly with these sentiments.

Materialism as not being the answer

From now, said Milligan, 'he had to surround himself with material gadgets to make him forget he was alone, but it never bought him a home [i.e., in any meaningful sense].' Now, in later life, 'he just keeps a small flat in London and the rest of the time he lives in hotel rooms.'[13] Said Michael, 'I think he was after inner peace, inner quiet, and he knew that you couldn't buy it. He must have by then because he'd been trying for a long time.'[14]

How Sellers hated the thought of ageing

'I'm not pleased with what I see in the mirror,' said Sellers,

> so that's a big drawback, I'm just disgusted you know. I think, ugh! I've got to go through the whole bloody routine of watching a bit more of the ageing process. There are many men like me, that belong to this strange brigade of pudding faces who melt in the crowd. Some of them sit in tubes; some of them are faceless.[15]

The limitations of Sellers' happiness

Said Milligan of Sellers,

> Even with his children he can only get a sad happiness. That's not radiant happiness. You don't go 'ha ha ha', the moment you see your children. You get a warm glow for something positive that's happened in your life. Peter does get that, yes. Perhaps these are the least unhappy moments in his life and so he classifies them as happiness.[16]

Chapter 26

Being There

In the year 1970, a book was published which was to have a profound effect on Sellers. It was entitled *Being There*, its principal character was 'Chance', and its author was Jerzy Kosinski.

Kosinski was born on 14 June 1933 in Łódź, Poland, to Jewish parents. He and his family survived the holocaust by living under false identities. He subsequently graduated from the University of Łódź, in history and sociology. In 1957 he emigrated to the USA where he graduated from Columbia University. He now proceeded to write several novels.

In 1971, said Kosinski, Sellers wrote him a letter

> saying that I had invaded his life. I met him, and I thought he was joking and for the next seven and a half years Peter Sellers became 'Chance' the gardener. He left his calling card as Chance the gardener, his stationery as Chance the gardener, and then one day he stopped me in Malibu in Hollywood and he said, 'You've got to understand, I *am* Chance, the gardener!'[1]

'Sellers was desperate to make this film,' said Bill Parnell, 'and had been for some years.'

The truth was that Sellers not only wished to acquire the film rights to *Being There* from Kosinski, he also longed to play the role of the book's principal character, 'Chance', and this became an obsession.[2]

The two men met in person in the mid-1970s in Beverly Hills, California. Said Sellers' daughter Victoria, 'my Dad and Kosinski hit it off really well.'[3] What finally persuaded Kosinski to allow Sellers to play the role of Chance was when the two men were strolling together through 'a mutual friend's sun-baked Malibu garden' and Sellers suddenly 'became' Chance the gardener in his mannerisms. This was Malibu, California, and the 'friend' was presumably, US film director, Hal Ashby. Said

Kosinski, Sellers' 'face was utterly serene. It was as if I wasn't within a hundred miles. He had stepped into his own world. He *was* my Chauncey [i.e., Chance] Gardiner.'[4]

As always, Sellers was meticulous when it came to his portrayal of the character and mannerisms of Chance. He 'couldn't get Chauncey's walk [right],' said Peter Evans, 'and he was struggling with this and one day Dan Leno said, "Peter what you've got to do is to walk this way" and showed him. But how he showed him, and how that manifested itself, I simply have no idea, but to Peter it was real.'[5] In other words, on this occasion, spiritualism came to Sellers' rescue. Another problem was to work out what Chance's voice sounded like. So, he said when interviewed by US film critic Gene Shalit in 1980, 'I spoke with an accent vaguely based on Stan Laurel [comic actor, writer, and film director].'[6]

The film *Being There* was directed by Ashby but Kosinski worked on the screen play and inserted several extra scenes. It was released in December 1979 and was a box office success. Kosinski described Sellers as a brilliant actor and 'a simplified man. He was actually extremely reductive. "Chance" the gardener is an actual Peter Sellers.'[7]

> Reductive: tending to present a subject or problem in a simplified form.[8]

Narrative of the film

In the film *Being There*, the cast is as follows: Chance – Peter Sellers; Eve Rand – Shirley MacLaine; Benjamin Rand – Melvyn Douglas; President Bobby – Jack Warden; Dr Robert Allenby – Richard Dysart; Vladimir Skrapinov – Richard Basehart; Louise – Ruth Attaway; Thomas Franklin – Dave Clennon; Sally Hayes – Fran Brill.

Chance wakes up in his bedroom in the big house, gets up, rearranges his beloved pot plants, gets dressed and dusts his master's motor car. Then he sits down to watch television, flicking from a concert, to a cartoon, to the news. Whereupon, Louise the maid comes in and announces, 'The Old Man's dead.' Chance reacts to this by saying that he wonders if it is going to snow. 'Is that all you got to say?' she says, and she goes off to make the breakfast. Chance remarks that he is 'very hungry'.

The action moves to the garden, where Chance is tending the plants and feeding the fish. Says Louise, 'You're going to need somebody. You ought to find yourself a lady, Chance. I guess it ought to be an old lady. You ain't going to do a young one any good, not with that little thing of yours. You're always goin' to be a little boy, ain't you.' Then she kisses him and says goodbye.

Chance sits beside the corpse of the Old Man, everything in the room being covered in white drapes. He removes one of the drapes to reveal a television set and resumes watching.

A Mr Thomas Franklin and Miss Sally Hayes arrive, representing the law firm which is handling the Old Man's estate. Chance tells them that he's waiting for lunch. 'May I ask just what you're doing here?' says Franklin. 'I live here,' he replies.

Chance declares that he has worked in the garden ever since he was a child, but when Miss Hayes inspects the inventory, she finds no mention of a gardener since the year 1933. In fact, there is no record of Chance at all. Was there any proof that he had resided here? 'You have *me*, I'm here,' says Chance.

Franklin admires the deceased owner's car. Whereupon Chance tells him, 'I've never been in an automobile. I've never been allowed outside of the house.' He then proudly shows Franklin his television set, 'with a remote control' given to him by the deceased owner. 'I'm allowed to go to the attic and wear any of the Old Man's clothes,' he says. Miss Hayes remarks that the particular style of dress that he was wearing was now 'coming back into style'. What sort of claim was Chance planning to make against the deceased's estate, asks Franklin? The garden was 'a healthy one', replied Chance, and he had no claim.

Franklin now tells Chance that he has no legal right to remain and will have to move out 'by let's say, noon tomorrow'. 'What about medical records?' asks Miss Hayes. Could Chance provide the name of his doctor or dentist? 'I have no doctor or dentist,' he replies. The following day, Chance goes up to the attic, fetches a trunk down and begins packing. He takes one last nostalgic look at the garden and then leaves the house.

Despite the grandeur of the house, this is an unsalubrious area of Washington DC, with rubbish strewn everywhere. When Chance asks a black lady carrying a shopping bag whether she can give him some lunch, she looks aghast and scurries away. 'Excuse me, can you please tell me where I can find a garden to work in?' he asks a group of black youths. Whereupon, they look at him incredulously.

One of the youths enquires, 'Who sent you here, boy? Did that chicken-shit asshole Raphael send you, boy?' He then pulls a knife on Chance and says, 'Now move, honky, or I shall cut your white ass.' Meanwhile, says the black youth, if Mr Raphael had anything to say to him, 'he should get down here in person'. Chance promises to give Mr Raphael the message. 'Don't show your honky face here again!' one of the youths shouts.

Chance goes on his way, pausing to admire a statue of Abraham Lincoln. To a policeman, he says, 'Excuse me, that tree is very sick. It needs care.' He now sees a television screen in a shop window, where his features appear on the screen, transmitted, unbeknown to him, by CCTV.

Chance's leg is crushed when a car owned by a Mrs Eve Rand (played with consummate skill and sensitivity by Shirley MacLaine) and driven by her chauffeur reverses into another accidentally. Eve offers to take him to the hospital. He is nervous about travelling by car, but he gets in and asks if he may watch television.

Eve has a change of mind and offers to take Chance to her home, instead, where her husband is seriously ill. Meanwhile, she offers him a drink from the car's drinks cabinet. She asks his name, and when he tells her, she misunderstands, thinking that he said 'Chauncey' instead of 'Chance'. As she chatters away in the car, Chance is only concerned with scanning the TV channels. She looks at him with curiosity as he watches ever noisier cartoons.

Chance is taken to the third-floor guest suite of Eve's enormous house. 'I've never been in one of these before,' he says, as he ascends in the lift. 'Does it have a television?' Having examined his leg the doctor, Robert, enquires of him, 'Are you planning on making any sort of claim against the Rands?' on account of the accident. 'There's no need for a claim. I don't even know what they look like,' replies Chance.

As Doctor Robert is talking, Chance finds the television's remote control and switches it on. Robert asks Chance if it is possible that he could remain at the Rand's house for a day or two, 'so we can keep an eye on you'. Whereupon Chance enquires, 'Does it have a garden?'

Chance is introduced to Eve's husband Ben, who is lying in bed in a room kitted out like a hospital ward, complete with X-ray machine. 'I've never seen anything like this on television,' Chance declares, as he has his leg X-rayed. Did Chance wish her to notify anyone about his situation, asks Eve over dinner? 'No, there was nobody,' he replies.

Chance tells his hosts that his house was shut down by the attorneys. Whereupon, Ben takes this to mean that the attorneys have also shut down his business, which is in fact, non-existent! When asked what his plans were, Chance replies, 'I would like to work in your garden.' 'Isn't that what every businessman is,' says Ben. 'A gardener. He makes a thing of value, for his family, for the community. A productive businessman is a labourer in the vineyard.' Believing that Chance is someone who has lost everything, Ben tells him, 'You can't let those bastards get you down. You've got to fight!'

They dine at an enormous table, waited on by numerous servants. There were thousands of businessmen both large and small in his situation, Ben tells Chance. 'We've been harassed long enough by inflation, increased taxation, all sorts of indecencies,' he declares.

When the Rands' concierge asks Chance if he would like a car he replies, 'Yes, I would like a car,' meaning that he would like to own a motor car himself. Whereupon a taxicab is ordered and an enormous stretch limousine arrives!

Doctor Robert tells Chance that the President, who is en route to the annual meeting of the First American Financial Corporation, has agreed to sit in for Ben, who is chairman of the board. Furthermore, the President will be arriving at the Rands' house shortly. 'Ben would like me to meet the President,' Chance tells the doctor. The Rands' house now swarms with security guards and dogs.

At 10 a.m. the President arrives in an enormous motorcade – with motorcycle outriders, flashing lights, and hooting sirens. Ben tells Chance that he admires his 'admirable balance. You seem to be a truly peaceful man'. In his enormous library, Ben introduces Chance to the President as 'my very dear friend'. 'I've seen you on television, Mr President,' says Chance. 'You look much smaller.' At this, the President is not amused!

The President asks Chance if he agrees with Ben, or did he think that growth could be stimulated by temporary measures? Chance replies, 'As long as the roots are not severed, all is well, and all will be well in the garden. In a garden growth has its seasons, first comes spring and summer but then we have fall and winter. And then we get spring and summer again.' Says Ben, 'I think what our insightful young friend is saying is that we welcome the inevitable seasons of nature, but we're upset by the seasons of our economy.' 'Yes,' says Chance, 'there will be growth in the spring.'

The President tells Chance that he regards what he has just said as 'most refreshing and optimistic. I admire your good solid sense. That's precisely what we lack on Capitol Hill.' They shake hands and the President leaves. Chance agrees with Ben that the President is a decent fellow. 'I'm glad he came,' he says.

Ben invites Chance to take charge of his scheme for financial assistance to businessmen. 'I think you're just the man to take charge of an institution like that.' He tells Chance that he is 'awfully tired'. Whereupon, Chance replies, 'I'm sorry you're so sick, Ben.'

Eve shows Chance her rose garden, containing some twenty thousand roses, and a greenhouse roughly the size of the Crystal Palace! Chance talks about Louise, and Eve is relieved when he explains that she was the maid at his former home, and not someone with whom he was romantically involved. 'No, she used to bring me my meals,' he says. 'She was very kind to me.'

In a speech to the nation, the President says of Chance, 'I've found Mr Gardiner to have a feeling for this country that we need more of. I thought Mr Gardiner the most intuitive of men,' he says, and he proceeds to tell his colleagues what Chance had said about 'the roots', interpreting this to mean 'the roots of industry'. 'Let us anticipate the rapid growth in springtime,' he says. 'Let us await the rewards of summer.'

Chance is told that the financial editor of the *Washington Post* is on the telephone for him. The next telephone call comes from the producer of *The Gary Byrne Show*. Would Chance be interested in appearing on the show, in the absence of the vice president? Meanwhile, Chance imitates the movements of a gymnast who he is watching on the television screen.

On arrival at the television studio, Chance is told, 'Of course, Mr Gardiner, your position in the financial community carries a lot of weight, but what caught Gary's interest was your down to earth philosophy. Do you realise that more people will be watching you tonight than all those that have seen theatre plays in the last forty years?' 'Why?' Chance enquires. 'Hell, I don't know!'

Meanwhile, when asked to do a background check on Chance, the security officer concludes, 'There is no information of any sort about Gardiner. We have no material on him, zilch.'

Even when he is being made up for his interview for *The Gary Byrne Show*, Chance watches television out of the corner of his eye. Says Gary Byrne, the host, 'It's always somewhat surprising to find men like yourself working so intimately with the President, and yet somehow managing to remain relatively unknown.' To which Chance replies, 'Yes, it is surprising.'

'I assume that you are inclined to agree with his view of the economy?'

'Oh? Which view?' Applause from audience. 'It is possible for everything to grow strong and there is plenty of room for new trees and new flowers of all kinds.' Further applause from the audience. 'The garden needs a lot of care and a lot of love, and if you give your garden a lot of love, things grow. But first, some things must wither, some trees die, and fresh young saplings take their place.' More applause.

'Do you feel that we have, in your words, a very good gardener in office at this time?'

'Oh yes,' replies Chance. 'Some plants do well in the sun and others grow better in the shade.'

'It sounds as if we need a lot of gardening.'

'We certainly do!' More applause.

Meanwhile, at her home, Louise is watching the interview on television. Referring to Chance, she says, 'I raised that boy. But I'll say right now, he never learned to read and write. No sir! He had no brains at all. Stuffed with rice pudding between the ears. Short-changed by the Lord and dumb as a jackass! Look at him now. All you've got to be is white in America to get whatever you want.'

Meanwhile, referring to Chance, Ben says to his wife Eve, 'You're fond of him too, aren't you?' and she nods.

Ben tells Chance that he would be doing him a great favour were he to stand in for him at a reception for the Soviet Ambassador, and also escort Eve. 'Oh Chauncey,' he says. 'You have the gift of being natural. That's a great talent, my boy. I hope the entire country was listening [to the interview], the entire country.' Eve gives Chance a prolonged kiss and walks off with a smile.

Meanwhile, 'I've been everywhere. There's no place left to look,' says the security officer. 'There's nothing. It's like Gardiner never existed!' However, the Bureau (FBI) did have some information. 'His suits [which of course were handed down to him by his former employer the 'Old Man'] were made by a New York tailor, handmade in 1928. The tailor went out of business in 1933 and later took his own life.' As regards Chance's underwear, the factory that made it 'was destroyed by fire in 1948'.

Chance is having his breakfast in bed and watching television when Eve comes into the room in her négligée. She tells him that he is described in the newspaper as one of the principal architects of the President's speech.

The President is 'a nice man', says Chance. 'You're very nice too', says Eve. She sits on the bed in an alluring way, but he continues to watch television. Suddenly, she pushes his breakfast tray back and engages him in a passionate embrace. 'You're so strong, I know I can trust myself with you,' she says, as he struggles with the television remote!

At the reception, Chance is asked what newspapers he reads 'I do not read papers. I watch TV.' A huge smile breaks out on Eve's face and she describes his handling of the press as being 'so cool and detached'. The Russian Ambassador tells Chance, 'You will find, my friend, that we are not so far from each other,' to which Chance, taking him literally, agrees. 'We are not so far from each other. Our chairs are almost touching.'

Because of a lack of information in regard to Chance, the next question for security is: what is it about his background 'that they're trying to cover up'? Has he a criminal record? Is he a member of a subversive organisation? A homosexual, perhaps?

When the Russian Ambassador recites fables composed by real-life Russian Ivan Krylov (1769–1844), in his native language, Chance chuckles, giving the ambassador the mistaken impression that he not only knows Russian, but is familiar with the works of the author to boot! Says Eve, admiringly, 'You had the Russian Ambassador eating right out of your hand, do you know that? I didn't know you spoke Russian, it's incredible!'

Chance is asked whether he would consider writing a book about his political philosophy. 'I can't write. I can't read,' he replies, but he is not taken seriously. The ultimate conclusion is that Chance can speak eight languages and has degrees in both medicine and law!

Security, ever suspicious, finally concludes that the only person capable of pulling off a stunt like Gardiner would be an ex-FBI man.

Eve confesses to Chance that when the time comes to say goodnight, she finds it very hard to leave him. 'It's very hard for me too, Eve,' he says.

Ben starts selling his stocks and shares in a big way 'so Eve wouldn't have to cope with it after his death.' 'There's something about him that I trust,' he tells Doctor Robert in regard to Chance. 'He makes me feel good. Since he's been around the thought of dying has been much easier for me.'

Chance is watching television as usual when Eve bursts into his bedroom and flings her arms around him. When she asks Chance what he likes, he replies, 'I like to watch, Eve.' She takes this to mean that he would like to see her masturbate! This she does, having told him that she is 'a little shy'. As she writhes about on the floor in orgasmic ecstasy, he remains preoccupied with his TV programmes. A female acrobat crouches on all fours and performs a handstand, which he attempts to emulate as he lies on his bed. The scene is absolutely hilarious. Eve tells Chance, 'Desire flows within me, and when you watch me my passion dissolves to desire. You set me free, Chauncey.'

On his deathbed, Ben summons Chance. 'Give me your hand. Let me feel your strength, Chauncey. I hope that you'll stay here with Eve. Take care of her. She cares for you. Watch over her, she's a delicate flower. So much left to do. I've spoken to my associates. They're eager, very eager, to meet you.'

When Doctor Robert announces that Ben has died, Chance says, 'Yes, I know, Rob. I've seen this before. It happens to old people.' Chance places his hand tenderly on the forehead of the deceased. He confesses to the doctor that, 'I love Eve very much.'

At Ben's funeral, the deceased is quoted as having once declared, 'I have no use for those on welfare, no patience whatsoever, and if I am honest with myself, I must admit that they have no use for me either.'

As the funeral eulogy is being read, Chance goes for a walk in the woods. He comes to a river. Holding his umbrella, and in the shadow of Eve's enormous mansion, he steps out into the water. He pushes his umbrella downwards, which indicates a depth of about three feet. In other words, he appears to be actually walking on the water! This sequence, of 'Chance walking across the surface of a lake' was inserted by Ashby himself, presumably with Kosinski's agreement.[9]

At the end of the film, as the credits roll, Sellers dressed as Chance is seen lying flat on a couch and laughing uncontrollably as he recalls the scene where the black youth called him 'honky'.

Being There gave Sellers a golden opportunity on two counts. Firstly, to play a role which he himself had chosen and thus prove that he was to be taken seriously as an actor. Secondly, to use this role as a vehicle for broadcasting his views (which he shared with Kosinsky) to the world on the western way of life.

The question is, what was it about the narrative of *Being There*, and in particular about the character of Chance, that Sellers identified with so powerfully?

Chapter 27

Being There and its Significance for Sellers

Being There and its principal character Chance struck a powerful chord with Sellers, for many reasons. As he himself said to Kosinsky, 'I *am* Chance, the gardener.'

The garden as a sanctuary

For Chance, the garden is his joy, his sanctuary, his solace, and his raison d'être. And the cartoons that he watches on his television also amuse him and are part of his cloistered world. As for Sellers, his mother had created around him an equally delightful, safe, and secure world for him when he was a child, and doubtless would have continued to do so had he not sought a female partner subsequently.

Chance's garden may have reminded Sellers of contented times spent in the gardens of his own marital homes, and in particular that of St Fred's, Whetstone, where he had been so happy, as his home movies testify. Here, he played with his children with unbridled joy, or delighted in the company of close friends. So, in identifying with Chance, Sellers' thoughts might well have returned to such scenes of domestic bliss.

The simple life

Chance possessed very little and was content to be in his garden or watching his television set. Expensive mansions, automobiles, etc., meant nothing to this humble gardener. Even his clothes were hand-me-downs from his employer. Sellers himself had known relative financial poverty as a child and also as a budding musician and entertainer, in contrast to the great wealth and 'celebrity status' that he attained in later years. And yet this had not brought him lasting happiness. For Sellers was never content, flitting from one wife or relationship, automobile, home, etc. to the next. As Milligan once wrote, with typical humour, 'Alas, Bentine is confined to bed with a severe overdraft, and Sellers is in America studying the plans of his next wife.'[1] Perhaps Sellers envied Chance his contentment.

Sellers and Chance: a case of mistaken identity as far as the world was concerned

Said Kosinski, 'Peter Sellers understood my character of Chauncey Gardiner better than I, for good reason. He has no interior life. No sense of himself. No notion of what he was or who he would like to become. He is, in fact, beyond definition by himself and entirely defined by society, which perceives him for what he is not.'[2]

But just as people misinterpreted the character of Chance, so the real-life public saw Sellers solely as a highly successful comedic actor. What the public did not see was a most unhappy man.

The sexual dimension

Just as Chance was seemingly indifferent to sex, so Sellers may have wished, in his darker moments, that he had been the same, considering how physical desire had led him into many a problematical marriage and relationship. Perhaps he imagined himself back at home with his mother, in his own 'Garden of Eden' provided by Peg, in those pre-pubertal days before sexual hormones began to mess with his mind.

Isolation

As an employee of the 'Old Man', Chance was isolated, except for the company of Louise the maid. Likewise, Sellers was comfortable only in the company of family and close acquaintances.

Sellers and Chance: both outsiders

Chance was never happier than when he was in his garden. Likewise, Sellers was never happier than when he was in the company of his family, or close and trusted friends such as his fellow Goons when, for once, he could relax and be himself.

Also, like Chance in his garden, Sellers, when at home or in *his* garden, was sheltered from the hypocrisy, unkindness, and rank duplicity of the outside world, which he had first railed against in *Songs for Swingin' Sellers* and *The Best of Sellers*, all those years ago. And yet it cannot be denied that he himself, as a famous film star in later life, became part of this avaricious, self-aggrandising, hedonistic, materialistic western way of life which, in theory at least, he detested so much. What had caused him to divert from the views he had held as a young man? Temptation, obviously. And why did he now choose to espouse them once again, and portray them vicariously through the character of Chance?

The most likely explanation is that as his health deteriorated, and he suffered with heart attacks, this caused him to embark on a reappraisal of himself. So, in his later years, he came to realise that money and possessions are no guarantee of true happiness. For had he not known great happiness with his fellow Goons, in the days when as a struggling actor, he had possessed very little?

Imitators both

Chance was an imitator of characters who appeared on television. Likewise, Sellers was an imitator of voices, par excellence!

Chance the nurturer

Chance the gardener realised that for his plants to grow they needed to be nurtured. Did Sellers regret the fact that he had not nurtured his own 'plants'? For example, had he taken more care to nurture the women in his life, then perhaps his relationships would have been more successful and fulfilling, and the same applies to his three children. Had he at last come to recognise his failings and inadequacies, and was playing the part of Chance in *Being There* an atonement, in which he was trying to make amends for previous 'sins and omissions'? However, when the opportunity did arise for him to put matters right with his children, whom he virtually cut out of his will for no good reason, he singularly failed to do so.

A colossal indictment of western values

When, on the death of his employer, Chance emerges into the outside world, he finds himself in an alien environment where values are based upon wealth, property, and status. So much so that whenever he speaks, instead of being taken literally as he intends, those around him think he is speaking metaphorically, and that his words relate to the US economy and US business. Furthermore, in this materialistic world, everyone is terrified of being sued, or of a legal claim being made against them, in which case they are likely to be deprived of their precious assets.

A ridiculing of the 'establishment'

As businessman Ben Rand, his wife Eve, the media, and even the President of the USA himself come to regard the humble and straightforward Chance as a sage, so they become more and more risible on this account! And this notion would, of course, have delighted Sellers.

The appropriateness of the title *Being There*

Said Walker, like Chance, Sellers 'had become a celebrity in a way he could scarcely begin to comprehend – just by "being there", it seemed, or presenting facets of himself on which others could project their feelings in a way that confused his image with reality.'[3]

A life dictated by chance

When Chance the gardener emerged into the outside world, his life was dictated by chance. Similarly, as Kosinski told US journalist and film historian Aljean Harmetz, Sellers, since his heart attack, 'sees his life as dictated by chance'.[4]

The satisfaction for Sellers in acting the part of Chance

Lynne Frederick would become Sellers' fourth wife. Says she of her husband, 'occasionally he yielded to the temptation of huge fees, then bitterly regretted it when he saw how he had exposed himself to working on subjects unworthy of his talents.'[5] But this time it would be different. Said Walker, Sellers felt that playing the part of 'Chance' would 'purge him of the coarse and exploitive roles he had taken in other films. He would finally achieve the perfection that had eluded him.'[6]

A rant against the western way of life

Being There, for Sellers, was a vehicle for heaping opprobrium on the western way of life and those who espouse its values, i.e. make money their god. However, if *Being There* was meant to be a rant against western values and western 'civilisation', and surely this is exactly what it was, it should be pointed out that Sellers for much of his adult life was part of this civilisation. He himself became extravagant, hedonistic, and selfish.

Hedonism: The pursuit of pleasure; sensual self-indulgence.[7]

Sellers was naturally diffident about revealing why he empathised so powerfully with the character of Chance. After all, if the Hollywood film industry was to become aware that he despised the entire culture that it represented (despite his being a beneficiary of its largesse), it is hardly likely that he would have been offered any extra further work!

Sellers and Chance: both uncomplicated human beings

Said Anne Levy of Sellers, 'I don't think he ever got anything out of life eventually. I find it difficult to watch *Being There*, because it is too near the truth.'[8]

Said Michael,

> The closest you will come to finding the 'real' Peter Sellers is to look at the character of Chance in his film *Being There*. The comparison is irresistible. To look further than that is a wasted exercise. Trying to read much more into Peter Sellers than there actually was has become many a biographer's pastime. He was far more straightforward than people are willing to accept.[9]

It is true that on a practical level, Sellers was basically down to earth and straightforward. With him, there was no conceit, pomposity, or airs and graces. But when his personality disorder manifested itself, he was far from straightforward: in fact he was unpredictable.

Louise's description of Chance

The maid Louise described Chance as having 'no brains at all', and as 'dumb as a jackass'. But surely this was to do Chance an injustice. After all, to be a successful gardener demands a knowledge of plants and the seasons. Likewise Sellers, who had little sense of self-worth, despite the fact that he was multitalented, may have seen himself in the very same light.

Conclusion

There is a saying that all roads lead to Rome, and in the case of Peter Sellers it might be said that all roads led to *Being There*. This was a film, the narrative of which had captured his imagination ever since he had first come across the book. In his portrayal of Chance in *Being There*, Sellers for once did not need to employ his wide repertoire of impersonations and accents because he so identified with and was in sympathy with the character that he was playing.

Chapter 28

Wife Number Four: Lynne Frederick (Married to Sellers 1977–1980)

Lynne Frederick was born on 25 July 1954 at Hillingdon, Middlesex. She was therefore twenty-eight years Sellers' junior. Lynne's parents were Iris and Andrew. When she was 2, her father left home and she was subsequently raised by her mother, who was a casting director for Thames Television. Lynne grew up in Market Harborough, Leicestershire.

Lynne was described as an 'English rose'. She originally intended to be a teacher of physics and mathematics. However, when she met Hungarian/US film actor and director Cornel Wilde, he invited her to star as Mary Custace in the film *No Blade of Grass* (1970), even though she had no previous acting experience. She therefore left school at the age of 15.

Lynne went on to achieve great success in the film *Nicholas and Alexandra* (1971), in which she played the second daughter of the Tsar of Russia, Tatiana Nicholaevna. She also played the wife of Henry VIII, Catherine Howard, in the film *Henry VIII and His Six Wives* (1972). In between times, she appeared in several television shows.

In 1975, Lynne declared 'I'd like to be a star but in the nicest possible way.' But this did not mean that she would 'automatically have to be boring, and late, and awful, and temperamental, and rude, and lose all the softness. I want to remain very much like I am, and not to get big headed and difficult.'

By now she had made 'seventeen memorable television appearances'; performed 'twelve film roles', and made 'two Oscar nominated pictures'. She also had 'a thriving modelling career' and an award for 'most promising actress to her credit'. However, her life was now to change.

Lynne first met Sellers at a Dennis Selinger dinner party in 1976. She turned down Sellers' first proposal of marriage, but after a year she accepted him.

When Michael first met Lynne, he said, 'her almond-coloured eyes to me shone with undisguised ambition.' He tried to reason with his father, telling him that if he married her and it went wrong he would be 'a laughing stock'. Michael also opposed the marriage on the grounds that there were 'twenty-eight years between them,' and 'his three earlier marriages had failed'.[1] Sellers took no notice and married Lynne on 18 February 1977 in the Mayor's Parlour in Paris.[2] He was aged 51; she was aged 22.

Sellers now purchased a villa in the South of France – for tax reasons. Said Michael, 'Dad loved the idea of a new home and a new marriage.' However, 'in times like this, we [his children] were a nuisance to him because we were part of his former life. We didn't really figure in his future.'[3]

On 20 March 1977, whilst on a flight to London from the French Riviera (where he and Lynne had spent their honeymoon), Sellers collapsed. He was admitted to London's Charing Cross Hospital and fitted with a heart pacemaker the following day.

Lynne devoted herself to being Sellers' wife and turned away the many scripts which she received for parts in films. Meanwhile, her husband's heart was beginning to fail. Lynne's duties included monitoring Sellers' blood pressure and also supervising his heart medication. 'Lynne was like a nurse to Sellers,' said his daughter Victoria. In addition to heart tablets, which included nitroglycerin, Sellers was also taking amphetamines to keep him wide awake during the day, and Mandrax (methaqualone) to help him sleep at night.

Bill Parnell, who met Lynne on several occasions, stated that 'she doted on his every word', and was 'desperately anxious to please him. And he, in turn, loved to make her laugh.'

How did Sellers' children view Lynne? Although she 'ran around after Dad, pampering him in every conceivable way,' said Michael, he could see that 'she wanted Dad to become totally dependent on her and indeed the power was steadily passing out of his hands.'[4] Said Sarah, Lynne 'seemed quite nice to begin with. She came across as very bubbly and friendly and warm and interested, but once they got married things definitely changed.'

However, 'I'm afraid we weren't very kind in our judgement of Lynne,' Michael admitted. 'Sarah thought she wasn't too bright.'[5] But surely, if the children had reservations, this was quite understandable. By that stage, Michael and Sarah had already had two previous stepmothers, and Victoria had already had one. As for their newest stepmother Lynne, she was born in the same year as Michael, and only three years prior to Sarah and only ten years prior to Victoria. Tensions within the family, and conflicts of loyalties on this account, must have been great indeed for the children to have to cope with.

Said Sue Adamus (Sellers' secretary, 1973–1980), 'He was ill, he wasn't old, but he seemed old, and she [Lynne] looked after him and had taken over very much the running of his life.' As regards Sellers' outlook, said Sue, 'I think a lot of it was fear: the fear of having to deal with things himself again and being alone again, and he had alienated so many people and he felt very much that Lynne was the one person in his life who was there.'

Meanwhile, Sellers and Britt were in dispute over 'Victoria's schooling and holiday periods'. This came to a head, said Michael, when 'Dad sent a letter to Victoria saying that she should no longer regard him as her father.' But instead of signing the letter himself, he got his secretary Sue Evans to sign it. 'When there was "dirty" work to be done it was poor Sue or Bert [Mortimer] who had to execute the deed.'[6]

In June 1977, Bert Mortimer received a letter dismissing him from Sellers' service. He was shocked. 'I couldn't understand it,' he said, 'and I still do not understand it to this day. After all I had given, and he gave a lot as well, but we also gave. I just could not understand why he would want to break a relationship, and even today I can't tell you why.'[7]

Lynne wished to have a child, but Sellers had become impotent. He explained this to Michael, in whom he now confided more and more. Sellers said he did not know the reason for his impotence, which was probably a side effect of his heart condition.[8]

Meanwhile, a rift developed between Lynne and her mother, who disapproved of Sellers because of the age difference between them and his poor marital track record.

Lynne was becoming more and more anxious to work again. Whereupon, Sellers invited her to join him in a remake of the film *The Prisoner of Zenda* (1979). He was to play King Rudolf IV and she Princess Flavia. This was to be the last film of Lynne's career. It was not a success.[9]

In summer 1979, when Michael married his secretary Carolyn Athay, Sellers attended the wedding, together with Michael's mother, Anne. (The marriage was of short duration and Michael subsequently married Alison Park from the USA.) In autumn 1979, Victoria commenced at a boarding school in Palm Springs, California.[10] By now, said Michael, his 54-year-old father was unable to walk further than 50 yards without 'panting for breath'. And yet he had signed for yet another movie, *The Romance of the Pink Panther*, in which he was once again to play the part of Inspector Clouseau. Alas, it was not to be.[11]

Relations between Sellers and his wife had become difficult. In regard to Lynne, said Michael, 'Dad was both pleading and acquiescent: ready to promise her anything if she was prepared to make a fresh start with him.' Lynne agreed, provided that he changed his will, which he did, signing the codicil in Paris on 29 October 1979.[12] According to the terms of the codicil, the children were to receive the sum of £800 each. Otherwise the will was entirely in Lynne's favour.[13] If Michael is to be believed, and there is no reason to doubt his word, this was tantamount to blackmail on Lynne's part.

By Easter 1980 said Michael, 'Dad and Lynne were uneasily back together, and they checked into the Dorchester Hotel in London.'[14] Against doctors' advice, Sellers now accepted the role of the doctor in *The Fiendish Plot of Dr Fu Manchu* (1980), with Lynne as an executive producer.

In spring 1980, when the family were on holiday in Switzerland, said Michael, Sellers showed a clip of the film *Being There* to Victoria. She told him, 'You look like a little, fat, old man in the part.' Whereupon, 'she saw Dad's face turn to thunder. Spinning round, he threw his drink all over Victoria.'[15] Sarah was the next to get into trouble, said Michael, when an interview she had given unexpectedly appeared in the *News of the World* newspaper. Whereupon, Sellers told her 'I shall be happy if I never hear from you again.'[16]

By July 1980, Lynne was living in California. Said Michael, his father was 'very, very lonely. I saw the desperation that imprisoned him,' whereas 'my own relations with Dad were now closer than at any other period throughout my life. I think Dad had recognised that I was not only his son but his best friend too. We could talk as man to man, knowing that there could be no breach of trust between us. The blood ties ran strangely deep.'[17]

A divorce was agreed, under the terms of which Lynne was to be granted the 'beautiful house' in Beverly Hills, California – for which Sellers had paid 'more than a million dollars', together with '50,000 dollars a year alimony'.[18]

'Four wives. What is wrong with me, Mike? Can't anyone understand me? Am I that difficult to live with?' Sellers asked his son forlornly. 'I thought I got it right with Lynne. I really thought she was the right woman.'[19]

Sellers retreated to the chalet in Gstaad in the Swiss Alps, 'that he and Lynne had chosen just before their separation. But Dad could find no solace there. Angry with Lynne, he struck her name from his will, leaving his entire estate to the British Heart Foundation.'[20]

But before finally signing the divorce papers, Sellers contacted Lynne. The outcome was, said Michael, that his father 'changed his will back in Lynne's favour': the changes being 'effectively made in a codicil signed by Dad in Paris on 29 October 1979'.[21] Whereupon Lynne flew to the French capital 'to be reconciled with him'.[22]

Chapter 29

The Death of Sellers: Aftermath

While taking lunch at the Dorchester Hotel on 23 July 1980, Sellers suffered yet another heart attack. Lynne returned to England to be at his bedside. He died early the following morning without regaining consciousness. This was the day before her twenty-sixth birthday.

Sellers' funeral was held at the chapel of the crematorium, Golders Green. Lord Snowdon, Baron Rothschild and Spike Milligan, Harry Secombe, and Michael Bentine all attended the service with their families; also David Lodge, Graham Stark, Blake Edwards, and his wife Julie Andrews.[1] Secombe described how, only a few days prior to Sellers' death, he and Milligan had planned for the three of them to meet for dinner. Now at the chapel, 'the four Goons [including Michael Bentine] were together for the last time.'[2]

At the funeral US trombonist and bandleader Glenn Miller's melody *In the Mood* was played. 'What was funny,' said Sellers' cousin Ray Marks, 'was that while all the wives were at the back crying, the [surviving] Goons were at the front laughing.'[3]

When Lynne learned that Britt Ekland was also in attendance, she was furious. 'Who invited that woman to my husband's funeral? How dare she do it? Why didn't she keep away?' she cried. Victoria was deeply upset by this outburst. Said Michael, 'I could find no excuse for her [Lynne's] tactless, hurtful outburst, and I left in disgust.'[4]

Sellers' ashes were interred at Golders Green Cemetery, which was the last resting place of his parents. This was in accordance with his wishes.

At the reading of the will, Michael learnt that his father's 'entire estate, apart from one or two minor bequests, was going to Lynne'.[5] The estate, valued at £4.5 million, included various properties, Sellers' art collection, family heirlooms and the rights to his films. As for his three children, they were left with a mere £800 apiece, and a message to them from their late father from beyond the grave telling them they must learn to stand on their own feet.[6] When he approached Lynne to see if she was prepared to 'amend things', said Michael, all she said was, 'Oh dear ... you poor things.'[7] After the memorial service, held at the Church of St Martin-in-the-Fields, London, the children did not hear from Lynne again.

These events caused a great deal of adverse press publicity, and Lynne was described in the press as a 'gold digger'. She finally turned to her mother, and after three years of estrangement the pair were reunited. Victoria subsequently challenged her father's will and was awarded £10,000 to pay for her school fees.[8]

Tributes to Sellers

The last time Lodge saw Sellers was during the making of *The Fiendish Plot of Dr Fu Manchu* in Paris.

> He was always terribly affectionate with me, and he gave me a hug and kissed my cheeks; but his nose was pinched, and he looked very ill. He died before the film was released, and they cut my scene out. He did behave outrageously at times and I did chastise him, but at the end of the day I had great affection for him. Apart from being my buddy I owe him such a lot – he cared.[9]

Said writer, director, and actor Bryan Forbes, after Sellers' death,

> I felt the loss of Peter as keenly as anybody and scarcely a week goes by without some fond memory of him surfacing. He was an emotional, perennial nomad, both on and off screen. Often I thought, consumed with doubts about his ability to sustain success, either soaring high on the peaks, or plunged in the valleys; there was no in-between.[10]

Said Hattie Proudfoot, 'He died a lonely boy, he was always looking for something that was not there.'[11]

Said Geldray of Sellers, 'We had a good friendship and I miss him very much. I was very fond of him, and we never had an argument in all the years that I knew him.'[12]

When Sellers died, said Secombe 'it was poignant for me that "Bluebottle" was "deaded" for the last time. There was no getting him back in the frame whole and ready to go again.'[13]

Said Milligan, 'I miss him very, very much. He was an irreplaceable part of my life, a wonderful part of my life.[14] Peter's nightmares are our nightmares too. His ghosts, our ghosts.'[15] Just before his father died, said Michael, he had said to Spike, 'I want to laugh again, I want to laugh just like we used to.'[16]

In November 1980 in an article in *Woman's Own* magazine, Lynne declared that 'Peter was unique, extraordinary, wonderful, and exceptional. He could love life one minute and hate it the next. He had always an aura of energy and excitement and he was never boring.' And in the preface to Alexander Walker's authorised biography of Sellers, published in 1981, Lynne wrote of Sellers as follows:

> I'll always remember Peter for a side of him that he only showed to those he totally trusted: it was a sort of sweet innocence. He had one phrase that sticks in my mind, the phrase 'I'm only a little thing', which he used to resort to when he couldn't cope, or when he felt people were out to get him, or when he blamed himself for something that had momentarily gone wrong.

This, she said, 'was an intensely vulnerable and disarming characteristic'.[17]

'He was a terribly vulnerable person,' Lynne continued, and 'people could "get" to him, hurt him, more woundingly than you could ever imagine. Peter never learnt to shield himself, despite his long years in the film business. People might think he was the toughest nut around – he wasn't; he had no protective shell. One word could destroy him.'[18]

Perhaps most poignant of all was what Sellers' loyal and faithful son Michael subsequently had to say. The television and radio, said Michael, were broadcasting tributes to Sellers, and 'people like Spike Milligan, Harry Secombe, and David Niven talked of their friendship and association with him. I felt proud of Dad; just why had he always thought he was so alone?'[19]

On 25 January 1981, only six months after Sellers' death, Lynne married media personality David Frost. Hollywood took a dim view of this and shunned her thereafter. Lynne suffered a miscarriage, and seventeen months after their marriage the couple divorced. In summer 1982, Lynne settled in Los Angeles.

On Christmas Day 1982, Lynne married US surgeon Barry Unger. On 29 July 1983 her friend, actor David Niven, died. She was distraught, having regarded him as her surrogate father. In 1991, Lynne and Unger divorced.

Lynne died on 27 April 1994, aged 39.

Chapter 30

In Conclusion

Why is it that we continue to find Peter Sellers so fascinating, in addition to him being humorous? This is for a variety of reasons. First of all, he was a consummately good comedic actor who, like his hero Alec Guinness, could assume virtually any part. He also had that wonderful sense of timing which for any comedian is an essential prerequisite. Who cannot help but smile at Sellers in the film *The Battle of the Sexes* (1959) in which, as Mr Martin, he looks out from behind the grille of his counting house at one of his clerks who is scratching away with his pen, and says, 'Mr Mickie, please can you find a quieter nib?'

Sellers' ability to mimic other accents – Indian, Scottish, Welsh, American – endeared him to people throughout the world. In the Clouseau films he was not afraid to make himself appear ridiculous. In fact, this was at the heart of the stories. Other films, by contrast, were intensely thought provoking, such as *Being There*, *Dr Strangelove*, and *The Fiendish Plot of Dr Fu Man Chu* (who was desperately seeking to discover the elixir of life). His facial expressions were the stuff of legends: that slightly twisted smile, sufficient to make one laugh even before the words emerged from his mouth.

On a serious note, as trade union shop steward Fred Kite, in *I'm All Right Jack*, he serves as a vehicle for parodying with consummate skill, the relationship between business and the trade unions, and in doing so, he was far ahead of his time.

> Parody: an imitation of the style of a particular writer, artist, or genre with deliberate exaggeration for comic effect.[1]

To discover the real Peter Sellers, the person that lay behind the façade, is not an easy task. In fact, he himself denied that any such entity existed. His real persona, he said, had been 'surgically removed'. He was an actor first and foremost, and even when he was being interviewed, he almost invariably put on an act.

However, there were times when he was candid, in particular in his conversations with Michael Parkinson, whom he addressed as 'Mike' and with whom he joked about 'bloody Yorkshiremen' – Parkinson being a Yorkshireman, as was Sellers' father, Bill. The two established a rapport and this enabled Sellers to be more open about his personal life than perhaps with anyone else.

And when we do find Sellers the inner man, whereas we might expect to discover an immensely happy individual, one who had in his time celebrity status: beautiful wives, immense wealth, magnificent motor cars, expensive yachts, a house in Mayfair, and various palatial residences, instead we find a person at odds with himself. In fact, Sellers the comedic genius, as portrayed in his films, is in marked contrast to the sad and dissatisfied real-life Sellers. And just as Inspector Clouseau battles against the odds, so we find Sellers battling with his wives, his children, the directors of his films, his fellow actors. No, for Sellers, life is always a struggle. He is plagued by self-doubt; ambitious, but never satisfied. And so he resorts to superstition, clairvoyance, and drugs to get through the day.

The truth is that when in the public eye, Sellers was desperately ill at ease; though he seldom revealed it. But once the mask did slip, and this was at the Cannes Film Festival, 9–23 May 1980, where he is recorded on film. By this time of his life, he was admittedly far from well. However, as he walks through a throng of film stars, directors, producers, celebrities, etc, with his smiling and relaxed wife Lynne at his side, he looks anguished, as if this is the last place in the world he wishes to be. As Bill Parnell said, when Sellers was with his coterie of close friends, he was relaxed and himself. But, said Mortimer in what was probably a huge understatement, he 'didn't particularly like to mix with strangers.'[2] And here at Cannes, in a rare unguarded moment, Sellers' true feeling were on display.

Although sometimes the stress that he was under, together with all the other features of his personality disorder, caused him to behave in an inappropriate and sometimes violent way, it is significant that the three wives who ventured an opinion appear to have borne him no grudge. Anne spoke of his low self-esteem and described him as the saddest person she knew. Britt admitted how much she had loved him. Lynne spoke of his vulnerability.

Furthermore, anyone who believes that Sellers was not capable of inspiring love and affection should hearken to the words of Spike Milligan, who said, after his friend's death, 'Goodnight sweet prince, may flights of angels watch over you.'[3] (This is a quotation derived from Shakespeare's play *Hamlet*: 'And flights of angels sing thee to thy rest.')

Of all the dramatis personae in the Peter Sellers story it is Michael who comes out with the greatest credit. For all that he had suffered at the hands of his father, with his unpredictable moods, irrational outbursts, and frequent rejections of his son, Michael never uttered a derogatory word about him.

Michael's biography of his father was entitled *P.S. I Love You*. The 'P.S.' may be interpreted in two ways: as being Peter Sellers' initials or, as it more likely, 'postscript', which was perhaps code for 'despite all'. But the words 'I love you' were undoubtedly sincerely meant. And Michael concluded his book by saying, 'At last we are a united and peaceful family and we bear the name of Sellers with pride.'[4]

At the root of Sellers' unease and dissatisfaction with life was a personality disorder, possibly inherited from his mother, Peg. And if this was the case, how ironic, that she, who had doted on her son and whose relationship with him was akin to that of a sycophant, was instrumental, albeit unknowingly, of passing on to him a trait that ruined his life. Peg, who had hoped to cushion him against the vagaries of fate, had likely planted within him the genes that were the seeds of his undoing.

Said Simon Williams of Sellers, 'he really should have been a bank manager. He had a very bourgeoise, ordinary, suburban set of values which was knocked haywire by him being a superstar and a heartthrob, and he couldn't really handle it. He was basically someone who needed to be working 9 to 5 and cleaning his car and playing golf on a Saturday.'[5]

Yes, it is possible that Sellers would have felt more comfortable and at ease out of the spotlight, but this would have in no way served to satisfy the ambition that burned within him. And, of course, had he not pursued his career as an actor, the world would have been deprived of the talents of one of the great comedic actors of the twentieth century.

But perhaps Sellers' greatest legacy is one that has not yet been fully recognised. In the early years of his career, the two gramophone record albums in which he featured poked fun at the establishment and its snobbery, humbug, pretentiousness, and hypocrisy. Latterly, the film *Being There* gave him an opportunity, vicariously through the character of Chance the gardener, to vilify the nastier aspects of the western way of life. Superficially a comedy, this film is, in fact, an indictment of so-called 'western civilisation'; of financial greed, political chicanery, racial disharmony and deprivation; social injustice and deprivation, over-weening materialism, the grotesque flaunting of wealth, and the worshipping of it as a god.

And yet it has to be said that for much of his adult life, Sellers was part of this very culture, being rich beyond the dreams of avarice, and also powerful in the sense that he could more or less dictate the parts he chose and how he wished to play them. But as he neared the end of his life, Sellers was evidently now looking back with some regret, and wishing that he had been truer to himself and to his core values.

Perhaps he had come to recognise the virtues of abstemiousness and self-denial, and perhaps this is what led him to experiment with Buddhism, and with the Hindu spiritual ascetic discipline of yoga. Perhaps he even had regrets about the ungenerous manner in which he had treated his children, right up until the end.

Perhaps Sellers is putting his hands up and saying yes, I could have led a better life, but instead I now give you the character Chance, as an example of someone who epitomised what I believe in in my heart to be the values that we should all aspire to: honesty, straightforwardness, and contentment with very little. Perhaps, deep down, he yearned for the simple life, that life, perhaps, which he had known as a child, and in his early days in the *Gang Show*, and with the Goons. And perhaps it was this yearning which prompted him to make nostalgic pilgrimages to places where he had previously lived and been happy, such as the garden at Brookfield, Elstead, Surrey.

For all Sellers' worldwide fame as Inspector Clouseau, his playing the part of Chance in *Being There* may be regarded as his magnum opus, his great onslaught, on behalf of the book's author Kosinsky, against the perfidiousness of materialism. When he was interviewed on the NBC *Today* show by Gene Shalit in 1980, Sellers was asked what *Being There* was about. He replied, 'It's Jerzy Kosinski's comment on power and corruption and the triumph of the innocent man: as Jesus Christ said, the triumph of the simple man over power, wealth, and corruption.'[6] Hence, the appropriateness of the final scene in *Being There*, where Chance appears to walk on water, just as Jesus Christ, the central figure of the Christian religion, had done following the miracle of the feeding of the five thousand.

Michael showed considerable insight, therefore, when he said that in order to understand his father, it was necessary to watch and understand the message of *Being There*.

What makes *Being There* such a great novel and film? Because, like so many important works of literature, it holds up a mirror to its readers and viewers and says to them, 'Look, this is who you actually are, like it or not! And this is the world that you have created for yourselves.' As for Sellers himself, when all is said and done, it seems likely that Chance was the kind of person that he aspired to be and wished that he had been.

Notes

Author's Note
1. Stevenson, A., and Waite, M., *Concise Oxford English Dictionary*.

Author's Preface
1. *Songs for Swingin' Sellers*, Parlophone, 1959.
2. *The Best of Sellers*, Parlophone, 1958.
3. Stevenson, A., and Waite, M., *Concise Oxford English Dictionary*.
4. The film *The Pink Panther* was produced by the Mirisch Production Company and distributed by United Artists. It was released in the UK on 7 January 1964.

Chapter 1 Who Was Peter Sellers?
1. *The World of Peter Sellers* (Tony Palmer Films, 1971).
2. *The Paranormal: Peter Sellers* (Blackwater Productions, 2002).
3. Secombe, Harry, *Strawberries & Cheam: The Autobiography of Harry Secombe, Volume 2, 1951–1996*, p. 7.
4. *The Paranormal: Peter Sellers*, op. cit.
5. *The World of Peter Sellers*, Tony Palmer Films, op. cit.
6. Ibid.
7. *The Paranormal: Peter Sellers*, op. cit.
8. Walker, Alexander, *Peter Sellers: The Authorised Biography*, p. 10.
9. *The World of Peter Sellers*, Tony Palmer Films, op. cit.
10. *The Paranormal: Peter Sellers*, op. cit.

Chapter 2 Sellers and His Father 'Bill'
1. Lewis, Roger, *The Life and Death of Peter Sellers*, p. 5.
2. *The Peter Sellers Story* (a BBC/Lionheart TV International Inc. – A & E Network co-production, 1995).
3. Sellers, Michael, *P.S. I Love You*, p. 27.
4. Lewis, Roger, *The Life and Death of Peter Sellers*, op. cit., p. 62.
5. Sellers, Michael, *P.S. I Love You*, op. cit., p. 26.
6. *The Paranormal: Peter Sellers* (Blackwater Productions, 2002).
7. Sellers, Michael, *P.S. I Love You*, op. cit., p. 28.
8. *The Peter Sellers Story*, op. cit.
9. Lewis, Roger, *The Life and Death of Peter Sellers*, op. cit., p. 67.

10. Sikov, Ed, *Mr Strangelove: A Biography of Peter Sellers*, p. 2.
11. *The Peter Sellers Story*, op. cit.
12. Sellers, Michael, *P.S. I Love You*, op. cit., pp. 27–28.
13. Sellers, Michael and Gary Morecambe, *Sellers on Sellers*, p. 27.
14. *The Peter Sellers Story*, op. cit.
15. Walker, Alexander, *Peter Sellers: The Authorised Biography*, p. 17.
16. Sellers, Michael, *P.S. I Love You*, op. cit., p. 26.
17. Stevenson, A., and Waite, M., *Concise Oxford English Dictionary*.
18. Sellers, Michael and Gary Morecambe, *Sellers on Sellers*, op. cit., p. 98.

Chapter 3 Sellers and His Mother 'Peg'
1. Walker, Alexander, *Peter Sellers: The Authorised Biography*, p. 13.
2. *The Peter Sellers Story* (a BBC/Lionheart TV International Inc. – A & E Network co-production, 1995).
3. *The Peter Sellers Story*, op. cit.
4. Secombe, Harry, *Arias & Raspberries, Volume 1: The Raspberry Years*, p. 187.
5. Stevenson, A., and Waite, M., *Concise Oxford English Dictionary*.
6. *The Peter Sellers Story*, op. cit.
7. Sikov, Ed, *Mr Strangelove: A Biography of Peter Sellers*, p. 9.
8. *The Peter Sellers Story*, op. cit.
9. Ibid.
10. Sellers, Michael and Gary Morecambe, *Sellers on Sellers*, p. 110.
11. *The Peter Sellers Story*, op. cit.
12. Sellers, Michael and Gary Morecambe, *Sellers on Sellers*, op. cit., pp. 111–112.
13. *The Peter Sellers Story*, op. cit.
14. Ibid.
15. Walker, Alexander, *Peter Sellers: The Authorised Biography*, op. cit., p. 40.
16. Sellers, Michael, *P.S. I Love You*, p. 57.
17. Sikov, Ed, *Mr Strangelove: A Biography of Peter Sellers*, op. cit., p. 153.
18. *The Paranormal: Peter Sellers* (Blackwater Productions, 2002).
19. Sellers, Michael, *P.S. I Love You*, op. cit., p. 37.
20. Sellers, Michael and Gary Morecambe, *Sellers on Sellers*, op. cit., pp. 98–99.
21. *The Peter Sellers Story*, op. cit.
22. Ibid.
23. Sellers, Michael and Gary Morecambe, *Sellers on Sellers*, op. cit., pp. 25–26.
24. Sellers, Michael, *P.S. I Love You*, op. cit., p. 57.
25. *The Paranormal: Peter Sellers*, op. cit.
26. Ibid.
27. Sellers, Michael and Gary Morecambe, *Sellers on Sellers*, op. cit., pp. 25–26.
28. *The Paranormal: Peter Sellers*, op. cit.

Chapter 4 Sellers Embarks on a Career
1. *The Peter Sellers Story* (a BBC/Lionheart TV International Inc. – A & E Network co-production, 1995).

2. Sellers, Michael, *P.S. I Love You*, p. 30.
3. Ibid., p. 32.
4. Ibid., p. 32.
5. *The Peter Sellers Story*, op. cit.
6. Ibid.
7. Sellers, Michael, *P.S. I Love You*, op. cit., p. 33.
8. Secombe, Harry, *Arias & Raspberries, Volume 1: The Raspberry Years*, p. 18.
9. Ibid., p. 189.
10. Milligan, Spike, *Milligan's Meaning of Life*, p. 120.
11. Ibid., p. 125.
12. Bentine, Michael, *The Reluctant Jester*, pp. 179–180.
13. Secombe, Harry, *Arias & Raspberries, Volume 1: The Raspberry Years*, op. cit., pp. 165–166.
14. Milligan, Spike, *Milligan's Meaning of Life*, op. cit., p. 126.
15. Bentine, Michael, *The Reluctant Jester*, op. cit., p. 197.
16. Secombe, Harry, *Arias & Raspberries, Volume 1: The Raspberry Years*, op. cit., p. 166.
17. *The Peter Sellers Story*, op. cit.
18. Milligan, Spike, *Milligan's Meaning of Life*, op. cit., pp. 137–138.
19. Ibid., p. 125.
20. Ibid., p. 125.
21. Bentine, Michael, *The Reluctant Jester*, op. cit., p. 218.
22. Sellers, Michael and Gary Morecambe, *Sellers on Sellers*, p. 131.
23. Ibid., p. 134.
24. Secombe, Harry, *Strawberries & Cheam: The Autobiography of Harry Secombe, Volume 2, 1951–1996*, p. 11.
25. Stevenson, A., and Waite, M., *Concise Oxford English Dictionary*.
26. Milligan, Spike, *Milligan's Meaning of Life*, op. cit., p. 267.
27. Norman, Barry, *And Why Not?: Memoirs of a Film Lover*, p. 117.

Chapter 5 Wife Number One: Anne Aspinwall-Howe (Married to Sellers 1951–1963)

1. Sikov, Ed, *Mr Strangelove: A Biography of Peter Sellers*, p. 55.
2. *The Peter Sellers Story* (a BBC/Lionheart TV International Inc. – A & E Network co-production, 1995).
3. Sellers, Michael, *P.S. I Love You*, p. 39.
4. Ibid., pp. 40–41.
5. Ibid., p. 42.
6. Ibid., p. 53.
7. Ibid., p. 42.
8. *The Peter Sellers Story*, op. cit.
9. Sellers, Michael, *P.S. I Love You*, op. cit., p. 43.
10. Sellers, Michael and Gary Morecambe, *Sellers on Sellers*, p. 46.
11. Sellers, Michael, *P.S. I Love You*, op. cit., p. 49.

12. *The Peter Sellers Story*, op. cit.
13. Ibid.
14. Sellers, Michael and Gary Morecambe, *Sellers on Sellers*, op. cit., p. 101.
15. Ibid., p. 52.
16. Ibid., p. 52.
17. *The Peter Sellers Story*, op. cit.
18. Sellers, Michael, *P.S. I Love You*, op. cit., p. 64.
19. Ibid., p. 64.
20. Ibid., p. 66.
21. Ibid., p. 61.
22. Ibid., p. 67.
23. *The Peter Sellers Story*, op. cit.
24. Ibid.
25. Sellers, Michael, *P.S. I Love You*, op. cit., pp. 70–71.
26. Ibid., pp. 71–72.
27. Ibid., p. 75.
28. Ibid., p. 76.
29. Ibid., p. 78.
30. *The Peter Sellers Story*, op. cit.
31. Sellers, Michael, *P.S. I Love You*, op. cit., p. 78.
32. *The Peter Sellers Story*, op. cit.
33. Sellers, Michael and Gary Morecambe, *Sellers on Sellers*, op. cit., pp. 102–104, 107.
34. *The Peter Sellers Story*, op. cit.
35. Sikov, Ed, *Mr Strangelove: A Biography of Peter Sellers*, op. cit., p. 57.

Chapter 6 Wife Number Two: Britt Ekland (Married to Sellers 1964–1968)
1. Britt Ekland, *Loose Women* (ITV London Weekend Television, 21 July 2016).
2. *The Peter Sellers Story* (a BBC/Lionheart TV International Inc. – A & E Network co-production, 1995).
3. Britt Ekland, *Loose Women*, op. cit.
4. Ibid.
5. *The Peter Sellers Story*, op. cit.
6. Britt Ekland, *Loose Women*, op. cit.
7. Sellers, Michael, *P.S. I Love You*, p. 91.
8. Britt Ekland, *Loose Women*, op. cit.
9. Pierce, Andrew, 'New Peter Sellers Letter on Marriage to Britt Ekland' (Telegraph Media Group, 31 July 2009).
10. Britt Ekland, *Loose Women*, op. cit.
11. *The Peter Sellers Story*, op. cit.
12. Sellers, Michael, *P.S. I Love You*, op. cit., p. 91.
13. *The Peter Sellers Story*, op. cit.
14. Sellers, Michael, *P.S. I Love You*, op. cit., p. 96.

15. *The Peter Sellers Story*, op. cit.
16. Sellers, Michael, *P.S. I Love You*, op. cit., p. 101.
17. *The Peter Sellers Story*, op. cit.
18. Sellers, Michael, *P.S. I Love You*, op. cit., p. 101.
19. *The Paranormal: Peter Sellers* (Blackwater Productions, 2002).
20. Sellers, Michael, *P.S. I Love You*, op. cit., p. 107.
21. Ibid., p. 108.
22. Ibid., p. 110.
23. Ibid., pp. 111–112.
24. Ibid., pp. 112–113.
25. Ibid., p. 113.
26. Ibid., p. 125.
27. Ibid., p. 126.
28. *The Peter Sellers Story*, op. cit.
29. Sellers, Michael, *P.S. I Love You*, op. cit., p. 161.

Chapter 7 Wife Number Three: Miranda Quarry (Married to Sellers 1970–1974)

1. Sellers, Michael, *P.S. I Love You*, p. 139.
2. *The Peter Sellers Story* (a BBC/Lionheart TV International Inc. – A & E Network co-production, 1995).
3. Sellers, Michael, *P.S. I Love You*, op. cit., pp. 142–143.
4. Ibid., p. 151.
5. Ibid., p. 152.
6. Ibid., p. 137.
7. Ibid., p. 144.
8. Ibid., p. 145.
9. Secombe, Harry, *Strawberries & Cheam: The Autobiography of Harry Secombe, Volume 2, 1951–1996*, pp. 14–15.
10. Sellers, Michael, *P.S. I Love You*, op. cit., p. 148.
11. Ibid., p. 152.
12. Ibid., p. 153.
13. Ibid., p. 165.
14. Ibid., p. 167.
15. Ibid., p. 167.
16. Ibid., pp. 168–169.
17. Ibid., p. 159.
18. Ibid., p. 159.

Chapter 8 Ambition: Talent: Humility

1. *The Peter Sellers Story* (a BBC/Lionheart TV International Inc. – A & E Network co-production, 1995).
2. Ibid.
3. Ibid.

4. Stevenson, A., and Waite, M., *Concise Oxford English Dictionary*.
5. Sellers, Michael and Gary Morecambe, *Sellers on Sellers*, p. 130.
6. Ibid., p. 166.
7. *The Peter Sellers Story*, op. cit.
8. Sellers, Michael and Gary Morecambe, *Sellers on Sellers*, op. cit., p. 149.
9. *The Peter Sellers Story*, op. cit.
10. Stevenson, A., and Waite, M., op. cit.
11. *The Peter Sellers Story*, op. cit.

Chapter 9 Getting Into the Mindset of His Characters
1. Peter Sellers: Interview: *Being There/Pink Panther* (Reeling in the Years Archives, 1980).
2. Ibid.
3. Ibid.
4. Stevenson, A., and Waite, M., *Concise Oxford English Dictionary*.
5. *The Peter Sellers Story* (A BBC/Lionheart TV International Inc. – A & E Network co-production, 1995).
6. Ibid.
7. Ibid.
8. Ibid.
9. Ibid.
10. Ibid.
11. Ibid.

Chapter 10 Sellers' Wonderful Sense of Humour
1. *The Peter Sellers Story* (a BBC/Lionheart TV International Inc. – A & E Network co-production, 1995).
2. Ibid.
3. Peter Sellers: Interview: *Being There/Pink Panther* (Reeling in the Years Archives, 1980).

Chapter 11 The Real Peter Sellers
1. *The Peter Sellers Story* (a BBC/Lionheart TV International Inc. – A & E Network co-production, 1995).
2. Ibid.
3. Ibid.
4. Ibid.
5. Ibid.
6. Ibid.
7. Sellers, Michael, *P.S. I Love You, op. cit.*, p. 14.
8. Stevenson, A., and Waite, M., *Concise Oxford English Dictionary*.
9. Sellers, Michael, *P.S. I Love You*, op. cit., Foreword.
10. Ibid., p. 43.
11. Ibid., p. 13.

12. Ibid., p. 45.
13. *The Peter Sellers Story*, op. cit.
14. Sellers, Michael, *P.S. I Love You*, op. cit., pp. 92–93.
15. Ibid., p. 94.
16. Ibid., pp. 115–116.
17. Ibid., p. 116.
18. Ibid., pp. 116–117.
19. Ibid., p. 141.
20. Ibid., pp. 119–20.
21. Ibid., p. 120.
22. Sellers, Michael and Gary Morecambe, *Sellers on Sellers*, p. 30.
23. Sellers, Michael, *P.S. I Love You*, op. cit., p. 193.
24. Sellers, Michael and Gary Morecambe, *Sellers on Sellers*, op. cit., p. 84.

Chapter 12 Sellers' Core Beliefs
1. Stevenson, A., and Waite, M., *Concise Oxford English Dictionary*.
2. Ibid.
3. Ibid.

Chapter 13 Generosity and Acts of Kindness
1. Sellers, Michael and Gary Morecambe, *Sellers on Sellers*, pp. 111–112.
2. Ibid., p. 135.
3. Ibid., pp. 135–136.
4. Sikov, Ed, *Mr Strangelove: A Biography of Peter Sellers*, p. 70.
5. Sellers, Michael and Gary Morecambe, *Sellers on Sellers*, op. cit., p. 123.
6. Ibid., pp. 172–173.
7. Ibid., pp. 173–175.
8. Sikov, Ed, *Mr Strangelove: A Biography of Peter Sellers*, op. cit., p. 305.
9. Ibid., p. 182.
10. Sellers, Michael, *P.S. I Love You*, p. 186.

Chapter 14 Nostalgia
1. *The Peter Sellers Story* (a BBC/Lionheart TV International Inc. – A & E Network co-production, 1995).
2. Ibid.
3. Sellers, Michael and Gary Morecambe, *Sellers on Sellers*, pp. 54–55.
4. Sellers, Michael, *P.S. I Love You*, pp. 153–154.
5. *The Peter Sellers Story*, op. cit.

Chapter 15 Some Notable Film and Stage Appearances
1. *Discovering Peter Sellers* (3 DD Productions, 2017).
2. Sellers, Michael, *P.S. I Love You*, p. 55.
3. Secombe, Harry, *Strawberries & Cheam: The Autobiography of Harry Secombe, Volume 2, 1951–1996*, p. 12.

4. *The Peter Sellers Story* (a BBC/Lionheart TV International Inc. – A & E Network co-production, 1995).
5. Bentine, Michael, *The Reluctant Jester*, p. 256.
6. *The Peter Sellers Story*, op. cit.
7. Bentine, Michael, *The Reluctant Jester*, op. cit.
8. Ibid.
9. Ibid.

Chapter 16 Insecurity and the Need to Escape
1. *Discovering Peter Sellers* (3 DD Productions, 2017).
2. Lewis, Roger, *The Life and Death of Peter Sellers*, p. xxxi.
3. Sellers, Michael and Gary Morecambe, *Sellers on Sellers*, pp. 117–118.
4. Sikov, Ed, *Mr Strangelove: A Biography of Peter Sellers*, p. 152.
5. *The Paranormal: Peter Sellers* (Blackwater Productions, 2002).
6. Stevenson, A., and Waite, M., *Concise Oxford English Dictionary*.
7. *The Peter Sellers Story* (a BBC/Lionheart TV International Inc. – A & E Network co-production, 1995).
8. Ibid.
9. Ibid.
10. Ibid.

Chapter 17 Low Self-Esteem and Its Possible Origins
1. *The Peter Sellers Story* (a BBC/Lionheart TV International Inc. – A & E Network co-production, 1995).
2. Ibid.
3. Ibid.
4. Sellers, Michael and Gary Morecambe, *Sellers on Sellers*, p. 107.
5. Sikov, Ed, *Mr Strangelove: A Biography of Peter Sellers*, p. 18.
6. Ibid., p. 152.
7. Sellers, Michael and Gary Morecambe, *Sellers on Sellers*, op. cit., p. 107.
8. Sikov, Ed, *Mr Strangelove: A Biography of Peter Sellers*, op. cit., p. 258.
9. Peter Sellers: Interview: *Being There/Pink Panther* (Reeling in the Years Archives, 1980).
10. Sellers, Michael and Gary Morecambe, *Sellers on Sellers*, op. cit., p. 186.
11. Sellers, Michael, *P.S. I Love You*, p. 86.
12. *The Peter Sellers Story*, op. cit.

Chapter 18 Sellers and Religion
1. Sellers, Michael, *P.S. I Love You*, p. 28.
2. *The Peter Sellers Story* (a BBC/Lionheart TV International Inc. – A & E Network co-production, 1995).
3. Lewis, Roger, *The Life and Death of Peter Sellers*, p. 813.
4. Stevenson, A., and Waite, M., *Concise Oxford English Dictionary*.
5. Walker, Alexander, *Peter Sellers: The Authorised Biography*, pp. 161–162.

Chapter 19 Sellers and Superstition
1. *The Peter Sellers Story* (a BBC/Lionheart TV International Inc. – A & E Network co-production, 1995).
2. *The Paranormal: Peter Sellers* (Blackwater Productions, 2002).
3. Stevenson, A., and Waite, M., *Concise Oxford English Dictionary*.
4. Sellers, Michael and Gary Morecambe, *Sellers on Sellers*, pp. 25–26.
5. *The Paranormal: Peter Sellers*, op. cit.
6. Sellers, Michael, *P.S. I Love You*, pp. 212–214.
7. Ibid., p. 63.
8. Ibid., p. 192.
9. Rhodes, Ella, 'The Everyday Magic of Superstition', *The Psychologist* (The British Psychological Society, November 2019, Volume 29) pp. 832–835.
10. Stevenson, A., and Waite, M., op. cit.
11. Vyse, Stuart, *Believing in Magic: The Psychology of Superstition*, p. 251.
12. Ibid., pp. 159–160.
13. Ibid., p. 160.
14. Stevenson, A., and Waite, M., op. cit.
15. Vyse, Stuart, *Believing in Magic: The Psychology of Superstition*, op. cit., p. 190.
16. Haupt, Angela, 'How Superstitions are Affecting Your Behavior', *U.S. News: Health:* 28 January 2014, online.
17. Vyse, Stuart, *Believing in Magic: The Psychology of Superstition*, op. cit., p. 159.

Chapter 20 Sellers and the Paranormal
1. Stevenson, A., and Waite, M., *Concise Oxford English Dictionary*.
2. Ibid.
3. *The Paranormal: Peter Sellers* (Blackwater Productions, 2002).
4. Ibid.
5. *The Peter Sellers Story* (a BBC/Lionheart TV International Inc. – A & E Network co-production, 1995).
6. Ibid.
7. Ibid.
8. Stevenson, A., and Waite, M., op. cit.
9. *The Paranormal: Peter Sellers*, op. cit.
10. Stevenson, A., and Waite, M., op. cit.
11. Ibid.
12. Sellers, Michael, *P.S. I Love You*, pp. 166–167.
13. Stevenson, A., and Waite, M., op. cit.
14. *The Paranormal: Peter Sellers*, op. cit.
15. Stevenson, A., and Waite, M., op. cit.
16. *The Paranormal: Peter Sellers*, op. cit.
17. Stevenson, A., and Waite, M., op. cit.
18. *The Paranormal: Peter Sellers*, op. cit.
19. Stevenson, A., and Waite, M., op. cit.

20. Sellers, Michael, *P.S. I Love You*, op. cit., p. 182.
21. Stevenson, A., and Waite, M., op. cit.

Chapter 21 Sellers and Spiritualism
1. *The Paranormal: Peter Sellers* (Blackwater Productions, 2002).
2. Milligan, Spike, *Milligan's Meaning of Life*, p. 261.
3. Stevenson, A., and Waite, M., *Concise Oxford English Dictionary*.
4. *The Paranormal: Peter Sellers*, op. cit.
5. Stevenson, A., and Waite, M., op. cit.
6. *The Peter Sellers Story* (a BBC/Lionheart TV International Inc. – A & E Network co-production, 1995).
7. *The Paranormal: Peter Sellers*, op. cit.
8. Ibid.
9. Ibid.
10. Ibid.
11. Walker, Alexander, *Peter Sellers: The Authorised Biography*, pp. 102–103.
12. Blake Edwards talks about Peter Sellers. FilMagicians, 2017.
13. Ibid.
14. Stevenson, A., and Waite, M., op. cit.
15. Vyse, Stuart, *Believing in Magic: The Psychology of Superstition*, p. 26.
16. Stevenson, A., and Waite, M., op. cit.

Chapter 22 Was Sellers Insane? A Personality Disorder?
1. Sellers, Michael and Gary Morecambe, *Sellers on Sellers*, pp. 143–144.
2. Norman, Barry, *And Why Not?: Memoirs of a Film Lover*, p. 111.
3. Blake Edwards talks about Peter Sellers. FilMagicians 2017.
4. *The Paranormal: Peter Sellers* (Blackwater Productions, 2002).
5. *Diagnostic and Statistical Manual of Mental Disorders*, Fifth Edition, DSM-5TM, American Psychiatric Association, p. 645.
6. Stevenson, A., and Waite, M., *Concise Oxford English Dictionary*.
7. Ibid.
8. *Diagnostic and Statistical Manual of Mental Disorders*, Fifth Edition, DSM-5TM, published in 2013 by the American Psychiatric Association.
9. Stevenson, A., and Waite, M., op. cit.
10. Ibid.
11. *Diagnostic and Statistical Manual of Mental Disorders*, Fifth Edition, DSM-5TM, American Psychiatric Association, pp. 655–657.
12. Stevenson, A., and Waite, M., op. cit.
13. Ibid.
14. Ibid.
15. Ibid.
16. *Diagnostic and Statistical Manual of Mental Disorders*, op. cit., pp. 663–664.
17. Ibid., p. 667.
18. Ibid., pp. 672–673.

19. Ibid., pp. 675–677.
20. Ibid., pp. 649–651.
21. Ibid., pp. 659–660.

Chapter 23 Possible Origins of Sellers' Personality Disorder
1. Bowlby, John, *Child Care and the Growth of Love*, p. 13.
2. Ibid., p. 13.
3. Ibid., p. 22.
4. Taillieu, Tarmara L., Douglas A. Brownridge, Jitender Sareen, and Tracie O. Afifi, 'Childhood Emotional Maltreatment and Mental Disorders: Results from a Nationally Representative Adult Sample from the United States' (*Child Abuse & Neglect*, Volume 59, September 2016) pp. 1–12.
5. Kairys, S. W. and C. F. Johnson & The Committee on Child Abuse and Neglect (*Pediatrics* 109:4, 2002), p. 2.
6. Stevenson, A., and Waite, M., *Concise Oxford English Dictionary*.
7. Ibid.
8. Taillieu, Tarmara L., Douglas A. Brownridge, Jitender Sareen, and Tracie O. Afifi, 'Childhood Emotional Maltreatment and Mental Disorders: Results from a Nationally Representative Adult Sample from the United States', op. cit., pp. 1–12.
9. Britt Ekland, *Loose Women* (ITV London Weekend Television, 21 July 2016).
10. Sellers, Michael, *P.S. I Love You*, p. 117.
11. *The Paranormal: Peter Sellers* (Blackwater Productions, 2002).
12. Sellers, Michael, *P.S. I Love You*, op. cit., p. 140.
13. Ibid., p. 199.
14. *Lynne: The English Rose* (Foster Hitchman, YouTube, 18 February 2019).
15. Sellers, Michael, *P.S. I Love You*, op. cit., p. 222.
16. Stevenson, A., and Waite, M., op. cit.
17. *Diagnostic and Statistical Manual of Mental Disorders*, Fifth Edition, DSM-5TM, published in 2013 by the American Psychiatric Association, p. 482.
18. Reichborn-Kjennerud, Ted, 'The Genetic Epidemiology of Personality Disorders' (*Dialogues in Clinical Neuroscience*, March 2010, 12:1), pp. 103–114.

Chapter 24 A Rollercoaster of Joy and Despair
1. *The Peter Sellers Story* (a BBC/Lionheart TV International Inc. – A & E Network co-production, 1995).
2. Sellers, Michael and Gary Morecambe, *Sellers on Sellers*, p. 116.
3. Secombe, Harry, *Strawberries & Cheam: The Autobiography of Harry Secombe, Volume 2, 1951–1996*, p. 9.
4. *The Peter Sellers Story*, op. cit.
5. Ibid.
6. Ibid.
7. Ibid.

8. Ibid.
9. *The World of Peter Sellers*, Tony Palmer Films, 1971.
10. *The Peter Sellers Story*, op. cit.
11. *The Paranormal: Peter Sellers* (Blackwater Productions, 2002).
12. Sellers, Michael, *P.S. I Love You*, p. 87.
13. Sellers, Michael and Gary Morecambe, *Sellers on Sellers*, op. cit., p. 107.
14. Walker, Alexander, *Peter Sellers: The Authorised Biography*, p. 139.
15. *The Peter Sellers Story*, op. cit.
16. *The World of Peter Sellers*, Tony Palmer Films, op. cit.
17. Walker, Alexander, *Peter Sellers: The Authorised Biography*, op. cit., p. 203.
18. *The Peter Sellers Story*, op. cit.
19. *The Paranormal: Peter Sellers*, op. cit.

Chapter 25 Why Sellers Could Not Be Happy for Any Length of Time
1. Sellers, Michael, *P.S. I Love You*, p. 85.
2. *The World of Peter Sellers*, Tony Palmer Films, 1971.
3. *The Paranormal: Peter Sellers* (Blackwater Productions, 2002).
4. Ibid.
5. *The Peter Sellers Story* (a BBC/Lionheart TV International Inc. – A & E Network co-production, 1995).
6. *The World of Peter Sellers*, Tony Palmer Films, op. cit.
7. Ibid.
8. Ibid.
9. *The Peter Sellers Story*, op. cit.
10. Sellers, Michael and Gary Morecambe, *Sellers on Sellers*, p. 161.
11. *The World of Peter Sellers*, Tony Palmer Films, op. cit.
12. Ibid.
13. Ibid.
14. *The Paranormal: Peter Sellers*, op. cit.
15. *The World of Peter Sellers*, Tony Palmer Films, op. cit.
16. Ibid.

Chapter 26 Being There
1. *The Peter Sellers Story* (a BBC/Lionheart TV International Inc. – A & E Network co-production, 1995).
2. Sikov, Ed, *Mr Strangelove: A Biography of Peter Sellers*, p. 356.
3. *The Peter Sellers Story*, op. cit.
4. Walker, Alexander, *Peter Sellers: The Authorised Biography*, p. 215.
5. *The Paranormal: Peter Sellers* (Blackwater Productions, 2002).
6. Peter Sellers, interview with Gene Shalit (NBC *Today Show*, FilMagicians, 1980).
7. *The Peter Sellers Story*, op. cit.
8. Stevenson, A., and Waite, M., *Concise Oxford English Dictionary*.
9. Sikov, Ed, *Mr Strangelove: A Biography of Peter Sellers*, op. cit., p. 364.

Chapter 27 Being There and Its Significance For Sellers
1. Milligan, Spike, *Milligan's Meaning of Life*, p. 200.
2. Lewis, Roger, *The Life and Death of Peter Sellers*, p. 546.
3. Walker, Alexander, *Peter Sellers: The Authorised Biography*, pp. 213–214.
4. Ibid., p. 214.
5. Ibid., p. xvii.
6. Ibid., p. 214.
7. Stevenson, A., and Waite, M., *Concise Oxford English Dictionary*.
8. Lewis, Roger, *The Life and Death of Peter Sellers*, op. cit., p. xxxi.
9. Sellers, Michael and Gary Morecambe, *Sellers on Sellers*, p. 92.

Chapter 28 Wife Number Four: Lynne Frederick (Married to Sellers 1977–1980)
1. Sellers, Michael, *P.S. I Love You*, p. 15.
2. Ibid., pp. 177, 179.
3. Ibid., pp. 180–181.
4. Ibid., pp. 190–191.
5. Ibid., p.177.
6. Ibid., p. 188.
7. *The Peter Sellers Story* (a BBC/Lionheart TV International Inc. – A & E Network co-production, 1995).
8. Sellers, Michael, *P.S. I Love You*, op. cit., p. 201.
9. *Lynne: The English Rose* (Foster Hitchman, YouTube, 18 February 2019).
10. Sellers, Michael, *P.S. I Love You*, op. cit., p. 204.
11. Ibid., pp. 220–221.
12. Ibid., p. 206.
13. Ibid., p. 207.
14. Ibid., p. 212.
15. Ibid., pp. 212–214.
16. Ibid., pp. 214–215.
17. Ibid., p. 218.
18. Ibid., p. 202.
19. Ibid., p. 201.
20. Ibid., p. 202.
21. Ibid., p. 206.
22. Ibid., p. 207.

Chapter 29 The Death of Sellers: Aftermath
1. Sellers, Michael, *P.S. I Love You*, pp. 228–231.
2. Secombe, Harry, *Strawberries & Cheam: The Autobiography of Harry Secombe, Volume 2, 1951–1996*, p. 2.
3. *The Peter Sellers Story* (a BBC/Lionheart TV International Inc. – A & E Network co-production, 1995).
4. Sellers, Michael, *P.S. I Love You*, op. cit., p. 231.

5. Ibid., p. 233.
6. Caroline Graham, 'The Girl Who Got Peter Sellers' £5m – and She Never Even Met Him' (*Daily Mail*, 8 February 2009).
7. Sellers, Michael, *P.S. I Love You*, op. cit., p. 233.
8. Caroline Graham, 'The Girl Who Got Peter Sellers' £5m – and She Never Even Met Him', op. cit.
9. Sellers, Michael and Gary Morecambe, *Sellers on Sellers*, p. 127.
10. Ibid., pp. 155–156.
11. *The Paranormal: Peter Sellers* (Blackwater Productions, 2002).
12. Sellers, Michael and Gary Morecambe, *Sellers on Sellers*, op. cit., p. 137.
13. *The Peter Sellers Story*, op. cit.
14. Ibid.
15. Sellers, Michael and Gary Morecambe, *Sellers on Sellers*, op. cit., p. 189.
16. *The Peter Sellers Story*, op. cit.
17. Walker, Alexander, *Peter Sellers: The Authorised Biography*, pp. xviii–xix.
18. Ibid., p. xiv.
19. Sellers, Michael, *P.S. I Love You*, op. cit., p. 226.

Chapter 30 In Conclusion
1. Stevenson, A., and Waite, M., *Concise Oxford English Dictionary*.
2. *The Peter Sellers Story* (a BBC/Lionheart TV International Inc. – A & E Network co-production, 1995).
3. *The World of Peter Sellers*, Tony Palmer Films, 1971.
4. Sellers, Michael, *P.S. I Love You*, p. 238.
5. *The Paranormal: Peter Sellers* (Blackwater Productions, 2002).
6. FilMagicians, YouTube.

Bibliography

Bentine, Michael, *The Reluctant Jester* (Bantam Press, London, 1992)
Bowlby, John, *Child Care and the Growth of Love* (Penguin, London, 1965)
Diagnostic and Statistical Manual of Mental Disorders, Fifth Edition, DSM-5TM, American Psychiatric Association (American Psychiatric Publishing, Washington, DC, and London, UK, 2013)
Lewis, Roger, *The Life and Death of Peter Sellers* (Arrow, London, 1994)
Milligan, Spike, *Milligan's Meaning of Life* (Penguin, London, 2012)
Norman, Barry, *And Why Not?: Memoirs of a Film Lover* (Simon & Schuster, London, 2002)
Secombe, Harry, *Arias & Raspberries, Volume 1: The Raspberry Years* (Robson Books, London, 1989)
Secombe, Harry, *Strawberries & Cheam: The Autobiography of Harry Secombe, Volume 2, 1951–1996* (Robson Books, London, 1996)
Sellers, Michael and Gary Morecambe, *Sellers on Sellers* (Andre Deutsch, London, 2000)
Sellers, Michael, *P.S. I Love You* (E. P. Dutton, New York, 1981)
Sikov, Ed, *Mr Strangelove: A Biography of Peter Sellers* (Hyperion, New York, 2002)
Stevenson, A., and Waite, M., *Concise Oxford English Dictionary* (New York, Oxford University Press, 2011)
Vyse, Stuart, *Believing in Magic: The Psychology of Superstition* (Oxford University Press, Oxford and New York, 2014)
Walker, Alexander, *Peter Sellers: The Authorised Biography* (Macmillan, New York, 1981)

Film documentaries

Discovering Peter Sellers (3 DD Productions, 2017)
Lynne: The English Rose (Foster Hitchman, YouTube, 18 February 2019)
Peter Sellers: Interview: *Being There/Pink Panther* (Reeling in the Years Archives, 1980)
The Paranormal: Peter Sellers (Blackwater Productions, 2002)
The Peter Sellers Story (A BBC/Lionheart TV International Inc. – A & E Network co-production, 1995)
The World of Peter Sellers (Tony Palmer Films, 1971)

Index

Adamus, Sue 121
After the Fox 25
Andrews, Julie 124
Anne, Princess 29
Ashby, Hal 103–104, 111
A Shot in the Dark 69
Aspinwall-Howe, Anne (*see* Howe, Anne)
Athay, Carolyn 122

Being There 2, 31, 33, 43, 99, 103–104, 112–113, 115–118, 122, 128, 131–132
Bentine, Michael 11–14, 16, 61, 78, 113, 124
Bentley, Dick 32
Boulting, John 62
Boulting, Ray 62
Bowlby, John 90–91
Boyle, Katie 75
'Brookfield', Elstead, Surrey 24, 60, 95, 131
Brouhaha 32, 61

Cannes Film Festival 129
Carmichael, Ian 35, 71, 75
Casino Royale 63, 71, 76–77
Carton House, County Kildare 28
Charles, Prince 29, 95
Chevalier, Albert 50
Chevalier, Auguste 50
Chipperfield Manor, Hertfordshire 17–18
Collins, Doris 9
Cooper, Gary 70
Crazy People, The 14

Dixon, Pat 13
Dorchester Hotel 23, 65, 93, 122, 124

Dr Strangelove, or How I Learned to Stop Worrying and Love the Bomb 62, 96, 128

East Finchley 8, 10
Edwards, Blake 28, 80, 82, 97, 124
Ekland, Britt 9, 23–27, 39, 57, 78, 89, 92, 96, 100, 121, 124, 130
Ellington, Ray 29
Elstead 39
Eton, Peter 14
Evans, Peter 2, 9, 71–72, 75–79, 96, 99, 104, 121

Fields, Gracie 11
Forbes, Bryan 7–8, 22, 101, 125
Frederick, Lynne 3, 63, 116, 119–127, 129–130
Frost, David 126

Gang Show 7, 10, 30, 64–65, 131
Geldray, Max 14, 29, 56–57, 125
Goodwin, Ron 47–48, 53
Goon Show, The 11, 13–14, 16, 29, 32, 35, 56, 95, 97
Grafton Arms 13, 59
Grafton, James Douglas ('Jimmy') 13
Guinness, Alec 32, 61, 63, 128

Hall, Peter 32, 61
Hampstead 21–22, 39, 71, 96
Handl, Irene 48–49
Harmetz, Aljean 116
Harrison, George 75–76
Haupt, Angela 74
Hayes, Anne (*see* Howe, Anne)
Highgate 16, 59
Hoffman 58

Index

Howe, Anne 16–22
Howe, Kathleen 16
Hudd, Roy 32

Ilfracombe, Devon 5, 10
I'm All Right Jack 35, 62, 95, 128

Johnson, Charles 91
Jones, Anthony Armstrong 57

Kairys, Steven W. 91
Kosinski, Jerzy 103–104, 114, 116
Kubrick, Stanley 34, 62

Laurel, Stan 104
Leno, Dan 79, 104
Levy, Anne (*see* Howe, Anne)
Levy, Ted 21–22, 59
Lewis, Roger 1–2, 4–5, 25, 75, 92
Lodge, David 64–65, 96, 124–125
Lolita 34, 62
Loren, Sophia 20–21, 68

MacLaine, Shirley 104, 106
Malcolm, Derek 61, 64
Ma Ray 4–7
Margaret, Princess 29, 57
Marks, Benvenida (née Mendoza, *see* Ma Ray)
Marks, Ray 124
Marks Soloman 6
McGrath, Joe 63, 77–78
Mendoza, Agnes Doreen ('Peg', *see* Sellers, Agnes, 'Peg')
Mendoza, Benvenida ('Welcome', *see* Ma Ray)
Miller, Jonathan 65, 68
Milligan, Terence Alan ('Spike') 1, 7, 11–16, 21, 29, 37, 56, 61, 66, 68, 70, 78, 95, 97, 100–102, 113, 124, 126, 130
Minnelli, Liza 30
Montagu Square 8
Morley, Angela 32
Mortimer, Bert 7, 22, 24, 28–29, 31, 58, 71, 75, 79, 95, 97, 121, 129
Muir, Frank 43, 51

Muppet Show 1
Muswell Hill 5, 16

Norden, Dennis 43, 51, 82
Norman, Barry 15, 82

Olivier, Laurence 32, 68
O'Toole, Peter 71

Park, Alison 122
Parkin, Hilda 11
Parkinson, Michael 5–6, 10, 54, 67, 96, 101, 129
Parnell, William ('Bill') 66, 103, 120, 129
Pascal, Françoise 57
Philip, Prince 29
Port Grimaud 72
Proudfoot, Hattie 8, 39, 65, 71, 125

Quarry, Miranda 28–30, 79, 92

Ray, Dick 4–7
Ray, Ma (*see* Ray, Belle)
Ray, Ted 11
Reader, Ralph 10
Red Cloud 79
Reichborn-Kjennernd, Ted 93
Rhodes, Ella 73
Roberts, Estelle 79, 91

Schreiner, Max 46–48, 53
Secombe, Henry Harry 1, 6, 10–14, 29, 35, 37, 61, 65, 95, 124–126
Selinger, Dennis 8, 10, 16, 61, 70, 75, 78, 119
Sellers, Agnes Doreen ('Peg') 4–11, 16–17, 26, 35, 37, 59, 62, 70–71, 77–78, 94, 101, 114, 130
Sellers, Michael 1, 4, 7–11, 16–30, 37–41, 58–61, 64, 66, 68, 70–72, 76–77, 89, 92–93, 96, 98–99, 102, 117, 120–126, 130, 132
Sellers, Sarah 17, 25, 37, 39–40, 89, 99, 120–122
Sellers, Victoria 25–27, 72, 89, 92, 96, 103, 120–122, 124–125

Sellers, William ('Bill') 4–7, 9–10, 16, 21, 67, 70, 90, 92, 94, 129
Shepperton Studos 62
Show Time 11
Sikov, Ed 5, 58, 64, 67
Snowdon, Lord 29, 124
Soft Beds, Hard Battles 63
Sommer, Elke 69
Songs for Swingin' Sellers 35, 42, 47, 54, 115
St Aloysius' College 59
Steve Allen Show 24, 96
Speer, Roy 32
Stark, Graham 7, 11, 29, 66, 124

Taillieu, Tamara 91
The Battle of the Sexes 62, 95, 128
The Best of Sellers 35, 42–43, 54
The Bobo 25–26, 28
The Fiendish Plot of Dr Fu Manchu 63, 72, 98, 122, 125, 128
The Ladykillers 61
The Magic Christian 78
The Millionairess 20

The Pink Panther 23, 29
The Prisoner of Zenda 3, 63, 71–72, 121
The Romance of the Pink Panther 122
Two Way Stretch 62

Unger, Barry 127

Variety Bandbox 11, 13
Vyse, Stuart 73–74, 80–81

Wachtmeister, Christina ('Titi') 30
Walker, Alexander 5, 7, 70, 79, 116
Welles, Orson 63, 76
What's New Pussycat 63
Whetstone, Barnet ('St Fred's') 17, 35, 113
Wilde Cornel 119
Williams, Simon 1, 3, 72, 82, 130
Wilson, Dennis Main 14, 34
Windmill Theatre 11–12, 97
Woodruff, Maurice 23, 75–76

Yarwood, Mike 33